George Eliot (Marian Evans)

Literary Lives
General Editor: Richard Dutton, Reader in English,
University of Lancaster

This series offers stimulating accounts of the literary careers of the most widely read British and Irish authors. Volumes follow the outline of writers' working lives, not in the spirit of traditional biography, but aiming to trace the professional, publishing and social contexts which shaped their writing. The role and status of the "author" as the creator of literary texts is a vexed issue in current critical theory, where a variety of social, linguistic and psycological appoaches have challenged the old concentration on writers as specially-gifted individuals. Yet reports of "the death of the author" in literary studies are (as Mark Twain said of a premature obituary) an exaggeration. This series aims to demonstrate how and understanding of writers' careers can promote, for students and general readers alike, a more informed historical reading of their works.

George Eliot (Marian Evans) A Literary Life

Kerry McSweeney
Molson Professor of English,
McGill University, Montreal

M
MACMILLAN

First published 1991

Published by
MACMILLAN ACADEMIC AND PROFESSIONAL LTD
Houndmills, Basingstoke, Hampshire RG21 2XS
and London
Companies and representatives
throughout the world

Printed in Hong Kong

British Library Cataloguing in Publication Data
McSweeney, Kerry 1941–
George Eliot (Marian Evans): a literary life. –
(Macmillan literary lives).
1. Fiction in English. Eliot, George, 1819–1880
I. Title
823.8
ISBN 0–333–48741–9
ISBN 0–333–48742–7 pbk

For Nick Sheldon

Contents

Preface

A number of general studies of 'George Eliot' have appeared in recent years. Most of them, like much of the more specialised attention her work has received during this time, divide into two principal groups: work with a feminist slant; and work chiefly concerned with the novelist's ideas and/or with the impact of social, political or natural science on her fiction. These studies have opened important new avenues into the George Eliot novels; but in doing so they have inevitably drawn attention away from other, equally important considerations, and in some cases over-emphasised the importance of their particular subject.

In what follows, the fiction of Marian Evans is placed in a biographical and literary–historical context. Since the life experiences that most influenced the novels were those of her formative years, biographical information becomes less important after the publication of her first novel in 1859, when she was in her fortieth year. I have endeavoured to give appropriate emphasis to my subject's intellectual development and ideas on the one hand, and to considerations of gender and sex on the other. And I have paid some attention to the poetry. But my principal concern has been with Marian Evans as a writer of prose fiction. I have, for example, treated in some detail her views on other novels and novelists, making more use than is usual of the numerous reviews of current fiction that she wrote during the mid-1850s. I have also emphasised her aesthetic thinking as it developed from the early celebration of the faithful representing of commonplace things towards more complex considerations. And I have called attention to the fundamental choices and presentational calculations that were made for each novel. At the same time, I have tried to identify and point up the distinctive temperament or sensibility that informs the novels – the particular quality stemming from the person of the artist that according to Flaubert every work of art contains within itself, and that affects the reader apart from the work's execution.

'George Eliot' was the pseudonym of Mary Ann or Marian Evans. She began spelling her first name in the latter way in the early 1850s; for the sake of consistency, I have used this spelling throughout. For the same reason, the narrator of each novel is referred to as 'she', despite the masculine self-references of the narrators of the early works. In an earlier book of mine on *Middlemarch*, the masculine pronoun was employed at the insistence of the general editor of the series in which the book appeared – a capitulation on my part that I came to regret even before the complaints began.

For quotations from the novels, I have used whenever possible the Clarendon Edition of the Novels of George Eliot. For works that have not yet appeared in this edition, I have used the texts in the Penguin English Library. Quotations from *The Spanish Gypsy*, *The Legend of Jubal and Other Poems* and *Impressions of Theophrastus Such* are from the University Edition of *The Works of George Eliot*.

In what follows, I have tried to keep in mind Marian Evans' own admonition that 'the scholar, who would produce a work of general utility, must not drag his readers through the whole region of his own researches, but simply present them with an impressive *coup d'oeil*'. But I have tried to indicate my indebtedness to the work of others, chief among them the late Gordon S. Haight, editor of the nine volumes of *The George Eliot Letters*, and Henry James, whose collected writings on 'George Eliot' fill over a hundred pages and who remains unsurpassed as a commentator on her fiction. I am grateful to the McGill University Humanities Research Grants Committee; Ruth Portner of Phoenix Books, Westmount, who lent me her collection of nineteenth-century biographical and critical studies of George Eliot; Stewart Cooke, who mediated my long-deferred encounter with word-processing; and my wife Susanne – as always.

Montreal
April 1990

List of Abbreviations

CH   *George Eliot: The Critical Heritage*. Ed. David Carroll.
        London: Routledge & Kegan Paul/New York:
        Barnes & Noble, 1971.

Cross   John Walter Cross, *George Eliot's Life as Related in her
        Letters and Journals*, 3 vols. University Edition of the
        Works of George Eliot. New York: Sully &
        Kleinteich, n.d.

Essays *Essays of George Eliot*. Ed. Thomas Pinney. London:
        Routledge & Kegan Paul/New York: Columbia UP,
        1963.

Haight Gordon S. Haight. *George Eliot: A Biography*. Oxford:
        Clarendon, 1968.

L   *The George Eliot Letters*. Ed. Gordon S. Haight. 9 vols.
        New Haven: Yale UP, 1954–78.

WR   *Westminster Review*.

1

Warwickshire 1819–1849

George Eliot was born early enough in the last century to see an England which has almost completely passed away, and yet her education was modern. Her youthful impressions were cherished with affection and were the root of a sweet and healthy conservatism. In later life she did not cast herself loose, but applied herself with all her natural strength and with all her stores of the newest thought to display and interpret the Warwickshire of her childhood, its fields, its villages, their inhabitants and their beliefs. It was not a mere outside London literary study, as those who remember the Midlands of her day can testify, and yet she was sufficiently aloof to depict them. She owed to them the foundation of what she was, but they, through her, became vocal. She was exactly the right person, and came at exactly the right moment.

William Hale White ('Mark Rutherford')

Marian Evans was born and lived the first thirty years of her life in the northeastern part of Warwickshire between Nuneaton and Coventry. The second half of her life was centred in London and considerable amounts of time were spent on the continent. But she always retained a deep attachment to the Midlands, and, imaginatively speaking, may be said to have never left. Six of her eight works of fiction were set there, and the display of provincial life and scenes is as fresh and copious in *Middlemarch*, her penultimate novel, as it is in *Scenes of Clerical Life*, her fictional début. A panoramic view of the region is found in the 'Introduction' to *Felix Holt*, which describes what could be seen in the early 1830s from the outside of a stage coach travelling through 'that central plain, watered at one extremity by the Avon, at the other by the Trent':

In these midland districts the traveller passed rapidly from one phase of English life to another: after looking down on a village

1

dingy with coal-dust, noisy with the shaking of looms, he might skirt a parish all of fields, high hedges, and deep-rutted lanes; after the coach had rattled over the pavement of a manufacturing town, the scene of riots and trades-union meetings, it would take him in another ten minutes into a rural region, where the neighbourhood of the town was felt only in the advantages of a near market for corn, cheese, and hay . . . The busy scenes of the shuttle and the wheel, of the roaring furnace, of the shaft and the pulley, seemed to make but crowded nests in the midst of the large-spaced, slow-moving life of homesteads and far-away cottages and oak-sheltered parks.

Her other novels contain numerous descriptions of more particularised scenes, some of which, like that of 'a pretty bit of midland landscape' at the opening of chapter 12 of *Middlemarch*, are rooted in the perceptual intensities of childhood and have a warmly retrospective glow:

Little details gave each field a particular physiognomy, dear to the eyes that have looked on them from childhood: the pool in the corner where the grasses were dank and the trees leaned whisperingly; the great oak shadowing a bare place in mid-pasture; the high bank where the ash-trees grew; the sudden slope of the old marl-pit making a red background for the burdock; the huddled roofs and ricks of the homestead without a traceable way of approach; the grey gate and fences against the depths of the bordering wood; and the stray hovel, its old, old thatch full of mossy hills and valleys with wondrous modulations of light and shadow such as we travel far to see in later life, and see larger, but not more beautiful. These are the things that make the gamut of joy in landscape to midland-bred souls – the things they toddled among, or perhaps learned by heart standing between their father's knees while he drove leisurely.

The paternal knees were those of Robert Evans, the estate agent for Mr Newdigate of Arbury Hall, who often took his youngest child with him as he went about the area conducting business. Marian's father had been born in Derbyshire in the early 1770s. He had been bred to the carpenter's trade and had little formal education; but, as his daughter later recalled, Robert Evans had 'raised himself from being an artizan to be a man whose extensive knowledge in very varied practical departments made his services valued throughout several counties. He had large knowledge of building, of mines, of plantation, of various branches of valuation and measurement – of all that is essential to the management of large estates' (*L*, iii, 168).

Like Adam Bede, the title character of Marian's first novel, Robert Evans had a younger brother, also a carpenter, who had become a convert to Methodism. Samuel Evans had married a fellow convert, who had been employed as a lace maker in Nottingham, where she had provoked a certain controversy because of her public preaching (it had been at one of her proclaimings of the love of Christ that Samuel had first seen her). She had also come into the public eye in 1802 when she had visited in Nottingham Goal a woman condemned for the murder of her child. She had stayed praying with her through the night and, as she later told her niece, 'the poor creature at last broke out into tears and confessed her crime. My aunt afterwards went with her in the cart to the place of execution, and she described to me the great respect with which this ministry of hers was regarded by the official people about the goal' (*L*, ii, 502).

In their later years, when Marian came to know them, uncle and aunt Samuel 'were very poor, and lived in a humble cottage at Wirksworth' in Derbyshire (*L*, iii, 174). Her mother's siblings, on the other hand, were as better off financially as they were different in religion. Robert Evans' second wife, Christiana, whom he married in 1813, was the youngest daughter of an established Warwickshire farmer. Her three sisters had all married well; like the three Dodson aunts in *The Mill on the Floss*, their religion seems to have 'consisted in revering whatever was customary and respectable: it was necessary to be baptized, else one could not be buried in the churchyard, and to take the sacrament before death as a security against more dimly understood perils; but it was of equal necessity to have the proper pall-bearers and well-cured hams at one's funeral, and to leave an unimpeachable will' (ch. 30).

Robert Evans had had two children by his first marriage; three more were born to him and his second wife: Christiana (Chrissey), Isaac and Marian, the last of whom began life on 22 November 1819 on the Arbury estate. Before she was a year old, the Evans family moved to Griff House, a comfortable, red-brick, ivy-covered residence in Chilvers Coton, which would be Marian's home for the next twenty years. There are close similarities between Griff

House and Dorlcote Mill, the childhood home of Maggie Tulliver in *The Mill on the Floss*. And there are other points of resemblance between the places of Marian's formative years and those of her early fiction. Arbury Hall, for example, the Gothic Revival castellated house of grey-tinted stone that was the home of the Newdigate family, is the Cheverel Manor of the second of the *Scenes of Clerical Life*, while the parish church at Chilvers Coton, where Marian was baptised and her parents buried, is the model of Shepperton Church as described on the first page of her first published piece of fiction, *The Sad Fortunes of the Reverend Amos Barton* (the first of the clerical-life *Scenes*), just as John Gwyther, the resident clergyman there during the 1830s, is the model for the story's unfortunate title character.

The immediate environs of Griff House – the rookery trees; the daisied fields; the cowslips, wild roses, lady-fingers, and forget-me-nots; the 'brown canal' (the Griff arm of the Coventry canal) – are lovingly recalled in the 'Brother and Sister' sonnets Marian wrote in the late 1860s. Their subject is the childhood intimacy of Marian and her older brother Isaac and the mutual influences on their young lives. Its theme is as central a concern in Marian's works as it is in Wordsworth's, her favourite poet and a major influence on her fiction: the lasting importance of childhood perceptions and experiences. The best-known passages in the novels devoted to this subject are the ends of chapters 5 and 14 of *The Mill on the Floss*, which speak of the sensory particulars of the 'home-scene' of childhood as 'the mother tongue of our imagination, the language that is laden with all the subtle inextricable associations the fleeting hours of our childhood left behind them', and which celebrate the stabilising influence in adult life of the 'loves and sanctities' that have 'deep immovable roots' in memory.

The autobiographical root of these passages is the sibling relationship celebrated in 'Brother and Sister', which describes two incidents that had already found their way into the novel: the sister's being frightened by gypsies and her catching a fish by accident. From their childhood ramblings the siblings

> learned the meanings that give words a soul,
> The fear, the love, the primal passionate store,
> Whose shaping impulses make manhood whole.

Those hours, says Marian, 'were seed to all my after good'. And she also speaks of the particulars of a vividly observed scene not only as having been part of her 'growing self' but as still being in the adult present 'a part of me / My present Past, my root of piety'. There is doubtless a certain selectivity and retrospective idealisation at work in these verse celebrations of 'the blest hours of infantine content'. As Marian herself observed at the age of twenty-three: 'Childhood is only the beautiful and happy time in contemplation and retrospect – to the child it is full of deep sorrows, the meaning of which is unknown' (*L*, i, 173). But in the novels there is nothing soft-centred about her fictional representations of early memories – the 'first affections' and 'shadowy recollections', as Wordsworth called them in the Intimations Ode, which have the power to become in adult life 'the fountain light of all our day' and 'the master light of all our seeing'.

The last 'Brother and Sister' sonnet opens with the terse report that 'School parted us; we never found again / That childish world where our two spirits mingled'. In 1825, at the age of six, Marian Evans was sent away to school; from 1828 until 1832 she was at Mrs Wellington's school in Nuneaton; and between 1832 and 1835 at the Miss Franklins' school in Coventry. At the first of these, Marian came under the influence of Maria Lewis, a young teacher of strict religious principles and intense evangelical ardour, who became her closest confidante for the next dozen years. At the Coventry school, the traditional, undogmatic, plain-speaking Anglicanism of the Evans home was exposed to a different kind of religious intensity – Calvinist theology with its emphasis on conviction of sin, hellfire and atonement. The Misses Franklin were the daughters of the minister of the Cow Lane Baptist Chapel, whose residence, physical characteristics and doctrinal ardour are all recalled in the depiction of the Reverend Rufus Lyon in *Felix Holt*. At the school Marian acquired a solid knowledge of English authors, won a prize in French, and learned to play the piano. She also lost all traces of the broad midlands dialect that her father spoke and that is so flavourfully recreated in the speech of many of the characters in her early novels.

Marian excelled in her studies in both the Nuneaton and the Coventry schools; but from the point of view of her future vocation, the knowledge of provincial towns that she began to amass during these years was perhaps her most valuable acquisition. The market town of Nuneaton was two miles from Griff. While at school there in December 1832 the future author of *Felix Holt* observed at first hand an Election Day riot in which two magistrates were injured, one person killed and troops had to be called in. Nuneaton is depicted under the name of Milby in *Janet's Repentance*, the third of the *Scenes of Clerical Life*. The picture is not flattering: it was 'a dingy town, surrounded by flat fields, lopped elms, and sprawling manufacturing villages, which crept on and on with their weaving-shops, till they threatened to graft themselves on the town'. There was 'a strong smell of tanning up one street and a great shaking of handlooms up another'. The Bridge Way, for example, along which rows of new red-brick houses containing ribbon-looms alternated with old, half-thatched, half-tiled cottages, was 'one of those dismal wide streets where dirt and misery have no long shadows thrown on them to soften their ugliness' (chs. 2, 4). When she sent the manuscript to John Blackwood, her publisher, he replied that he 'should have liked a pleasanter picture. Surely the colours are a little harsh for a sketch of English County Town life only 25 years ago'. In her reply, the fledgling author defended her representation: 'Everything is softened from the fact . . . The real town was more vicious than my Milby'; and the real Dempster, the alcoholic lawyer and wife-beater, 'was far more disgusting than mine'. And the clerical part of the story, which concerns the harsh treatment accorded an Evangelical minister who attempts to revivify the dormant spiritual life of the town, was 'a real bit in the religious history of England' (*L*, ii, 344, 347).

Coventry, eight miles south of Nuneaton, was a considerably larger town. In addition to her observations during her years at school there, Marian acquired further first-hand knowledge of the town after 1841, when she and her father moved to a semi-detached villa at Foleshill on its outskirts and she became friendly with the family of Charles Bray, a well-to-do ribbon manufacturer who was active in municipal affairs. In the early 1830s, when she first resided there, Coventry had a population of under 30 000. A journey to London took over ten hours by passenger coach (the time was to be cut to six hours when the London and Birmingham Railway opened in 1838). There was no proper hospital: both institutions for the treatment of the ill were for out-patients only. Public health also suffered from the lack of a main sewerage system, an inadequate water supply, and the condition of the burial grounds, which were located in the town's centre. Sanitary conditions began to improve in the later 1830s as a result of the Municipal Corporations Act and the publication of Charles Bray's pamphlet, *The Education of the Body*.

Most of the inhabitants of Coventry earned their living in their own homes making silk ribbons or watches. The traditional cottage-industry arrangement was vulnerable to market fluctuations and technological innovation, and when in 1831 a manufacturer began to use steam to power his Jacquard looms, his factory was burned down by a mob. Nonetheless, according to John Prest in *The Industrial Revolution in Coventry*, in the early 1830s the town still epitomised the old order, in which there were many ranks and conditions of men within a single, homogenous society. This is the society depicted in the greatest George Eliot novel, *Middlemarch: A Study of Provincial Life* (1871–72), which is set in the period between 1829 and 1832. Prest is only one of the professional historians who have attested to the historical value of the novel's representation of old provincial society:

The novel is historically accurate, not in the sense that individual characters can be identified, but in its nice sense of the distinctions between ranks, and of the links that still held the different ranks together in a single society. There is a faithful representation of the line between county and manufacturing families, and of the gulf between the old manufacturers and those in retail trade. The relationship of the country villages to the town is accurately portrayed, with weaving and squalor in the villages on one side . . . and agriculture and prosperity in the villages on the other. Above all, however, George Eliot with her philosophy, and with her acute perception of the way in which men have to suffer for each other's sins, was ideally suited to discover and to describe the elusive currents of public opinion which determined the standards of conduct in an old provincial town . . . In *Middlemarch* George Eliot has laid a large part of Coventry society bare to the roots.[1]

Marian Evans left the Miss Franklins' school in 1835, having been called home to be with her family during the terminal illness of her mother, who died early in the following year. After her elder sister married in 1837, the future novelist became her father's housekeeper, a position she filled for the next twelve years, first at Griff and then at Foleshill. One conspicuous feature of Marian's life at Griff during the later 1830s was its religious intensity. Sometime during her sixteenth year, while still at school in Coventry, Evangelical Christianity came to have a powerful hold on her emotions, which it continued to exert until she was twenty-two. 'I was then', she later recalled, 'strongly under the influence of Evangelical belief, and earnestly endeavouring to shape this anomalous English Christian life of ours into some consistency with the spirit and simple verbal tenor of the New Testament' (L, iii, 174).

During this period, her intensities and austerities were such that she 'sacrificed the cultivation of her intellect, and a proper regard to personal appearance'. She recalled that she used 'to go about like an owl, to the great disgust of my brother', whom she attempted to deny 'quite lawful amusements' (Cross, i, 116). During a visit to London she refused to attend the theatre and spent her evenings reading Josephus' *History of the Jews*. And her comment on an oratorio she attended was that musical embellishment was not 'consistent with millenial holiness . . . nothing can justify the using of an intensely interesting and solemn passage of Scripture as a rope-dancer uses her rope' (L, i, 9). The devising of a chronological chart of ecclesiastical history and the reading of theological tomes were activities more consistent with millennial holiness. So were her acts of charity. Marian organised a clothing club for families of unemployed weavers and regularly visited the cottages of the poor and sick. Like Dorothea Brooke in *Middlemarch* at the same age, she may have suddenly knelt down 'on a brick floor by the side of a sick labourer and prayed fervidly as if she thought herself living in the time of the Apostles' (ch. 1). But the quintessential characteristic of Marian's religious zeal was an intense concern with her own spiritual hygiene and an intense desire to be filled with the divine spirit. As her nineteenth birthday approached, she hoped that it would be an awakening signal and prayed that the Lord might vouchsafe her 'such an insight into what is truly good and such realizing views of an approaching eternity, that I may not rest contented with making Christianity a mere addendum to my pursuits, or with tacking it as a fringe to my garments. May I seek to be sanctified wholly' (L, i, 12).

In his biography Gordon Haight observed that if Marian's 'kind of evangelical severity had not been endemic and increasing [during the period], one might be tempted to look for psychological explanations – a feeling of guilt over the death of her mother that demanded punishment, and so on; the very paucity of comment about her mother is suspicious, and the period of renunciation and asceticism was prolonged till she was past twenty'. Such speculations, however, are immediately pronounced 'futile; one can only tell the facts' (Haight, 22). As we shall see, one can do somewhat more than this without becoming unduly conjectural if the continuities are emphasised between Marian's inner life during the 1830s and that same life during the next decade, after she had lost her religious faith. One must also remember that 'facts' relating to her 'evangelical severity' are available in unrepresentative abundance. This is because most of Marian's surviving letters from this period are those to Maria Lewis, her spiritual confidante and kindred otherworldly spirit. But there is enough evidence in other places to make it clear that those late adolescent years when she was her father's housekeeper at Griff were less exclusively given over to self-abnegating spiritual pursuits than they might seem to have been.

In one letter, Marian describes herself as 'so plunged in an abyss of books, preserves and sundry *important trivialities*' that she cannot write a proper letter (*L*, i, 57). The preserves included currant jelly and a conserve of damson plums. The important trivialities included sewing, the management of servants and social duties of various sorts. There was also a dairy to oversee that was presumably kept as clean as the one described in chapter 7 of *Adam Bede* and that may equally be thought to have produced the same 'real farmhouse cream' celebrated in the first chapter of *Amos Barton*. In later years, to remember the dairy at Griff Marian had only to look at her hands, the right one of which was broader across than the left because of the quantity of butter and cheese she had made while housekeeper there.

As for books, they were by no means restricted to moral and theological subjects. Indeed, it was during these years that Marian completed the foundation of the imposing erudition that is so conspicuous a feature of her novels. She had access to the library at Arbury Hall and her father allowed her to purchase any books she wanted. These included the texts that enabled her to satisfy 'the fascinations that the study of languages has for my capricious mind' (*L*, 1, 51). This interest that was further abetted by the employment of a Signor Brezzi, who came from Coventry to teach her German, French and Italian, and a clerical tutor with whom she read Latin and Greek. She also read books on historical and scientific subjects, as well as a great deal of poetry, especially that of the Romantics. On her twentieth birthday, she reported to Maria Lewis that she had been so self-indulgent as to acquire Moxon's new six-volume edition of Wordsworth. When she says that she could wish to have found in the poems 'an indication of less satisfaction in terrene objects' a more frequent upturning of the soul's eye', the remark seems as programmatic as it is gratuitous. But it is excitement and delight that one senses in the following comment: 'I never before met with so many of my own feelings, expressed just as I could like them' (*L*, i, 34).

One big lack in Marian's life during the later 1830s was a circle of friends with whom she could share her emerging intellectual and literary interests. This began to be remedied after she and her father moved to Foleshill in 1841 and became acquainted with the family of Charles Bray. Marian was soon on intimate terms with Bray, his wife Caroline and her sister Sara Hennell. They would remain her closest friends during the next decade, and Sara, who lived away from Coventry, soon supplanted Maria Lewis as her principal correspondent. And through her frequent visits to Rosehill, the Bray's home, she met a number of persons connected with the world of ideas and reforming causes.

By the time Marian came to know him, Charles Bray had put behind him the orthodox Christianity of his early years and become a freethinker. He espoused deterministic views, regarding the mind and personality as subject to the same inexorable rules as those governing the physical world. These views were expounded in his *Philosophy of Necessity; or, the Law of Consequences as Applicable to Mental, Moral and Social Science* (1841). He had also become an advocate of the then new pseudo-science of phrenology, which claimed that an individual's mental and moral characteristics could be ascertained by a study of the configurations of the skull.

Unlike their brother, Caroline Bray and Sara Hennell were serious believers. Indeed, at the time of her marriage, Caroline had been so disturbed by her husband's views that she had appealed to her brother Charles Christian Hennell, a London merchant, to re-examine the New Testament for evidence to support their faith. The result had been a remarkable volume, *An Inquiry concerning the Origin of Christianity*, first published in 1838, which so impressed the German biblical scholar David Friedrich Strauss that he arranged for its translation into German. In his preface, Hennell explained that he had begun his investigation in the expectation 'that, at least, the principal miraculous facts supposed to lie at the foundation of Christianity would be found to be impregnable'. But he had gradually become convinced that the life of Jesus Christ and the spread of his religion contained 'no deviation from the known laws of nature' and that the Bible contained no grounds for belief in the supernatural or miraculous origin of Christianity. In the *Inquiry*, all aspects of the New Testament story were shown to have an historical or psychological explanation. In his 'Concluding Reflections' Hennell asked what remained of Christianity once 'the miraculous birth, works, resurrection, and ascension of Christ' were 'classed amongst the fables of an obscure age'. The answer was that Christianity 'forms a striking passage in the history of human nature, and appears as one of the most prominent of the means employed in its improvement . . . It has presented to the world a system of moral excellence', and in its consolidation of moral and religious sentiments, it has 'constituted an engine which has worked powerfully towards humanizing and civilizing the world'. But Christianity was 'pre-eminently the religion of adversity' and how could such a retrospect be expected to console and sustain the afflicted? What could compensate them 'for the loss of the assurance of those mansions where Jesus is preparing a place for them?' The answer seemed to lie in a melioristic belief in 'the slow progress of the [human] race towards perfection'. As yet, science and philosophy were still in their infancy, 'especially as regards their application to subjects supposed to be connected with morality and religion . . . mankind may yet reach points in moral discovery which at present would at once be pronounced visionary'.[2]

Marian Evans bought a copy of the second edition of the *Inquiry* shortly after she came to know the Brays. She was much impressed by the book and read it a second time not long after. There is no doubt that Hennell's book, together with Bray's *Philosophy of Necessity*, helped precipitate her sudden-seeming loss of faith at the end of 1841, when she ended a letter to Maria Lewis with a reference not to God but to 'the sure laws of consequence'. And in January of the new year Robert Evans tersely noted in his diary that on two Sundays Marian 'did not go to church' (*L*, i, 124). But as a contemporary witness later recalled, Marian's passage from belief to unbelief was 'more gradual in its development, as well as deeper in its character' than might have been inferred from the collocation of her reading of Hennell and Bray and her refusal to attend church. The same witness (Mary Sibree, whose family knew Marian well at the time) reported that when later asked 'to what influence she attributed the first unsettlement of her orthodox views', Marian 'quickly made answer: "Oh, Walter Scott's"'

(Cross, i, 360). On another occasion during her adolescence, she had been disturbed by the impression given by a Bulwer Lytton novel that 'religion was not a requisite to moral excellence' (*L*, i, 45); and one may infer that a similar disturbance was caused by Scott's novels, which show there to be little correspondence between a particular religious belief and a particular type of moral character.

What this and other evidence suggests is that Marian's loss of faith was gradual rather than catastrophic and caused not so much by biblical scholarship *per se* as by widening intellectual and ethical horizons. Just such a conflict between the ethical implications of traditional Christian doctrines and a 'meliorist ethical bias' was not untypical of the period. All brands of Christian orthodoxy 'revolved around the same set of interrelated doctrines – Original Sin, Reprobation, Baptismal Regeneration, Vicarious Atonement, Eternal Punishment': and their lowest common denominator was the belief 'that this life is significant only as a preparation for the next'.[3] Once released from the grip of these doctrines, one was free to see (in the closing words of Hennell's preface to the second edition of the *Inquiry*) that 'theological belief, even of the simplest kind, and benevolence, do not necessarily exist in proportion to each other' and that what 'irresistibly demands our sympathies [is] a devotion to the cause of happiness on this earth'.[4]

Marian's refusal to attend church precipitated a crisis in her relations with her father. In a letter to him, she tried to explain her position: 'I could not without vile hypocrisy and a miserable truckling to the smile of the world for the sake of my supposed interests, profess to join in worship which I wholly disapprove. This and *this alone* I will not do even for your sake – anything else however painful I would cheerfully brave to give you a moment's joy' (*L*, i, 129). Her greatest fear, that her action would lead to a permanent separation, was almost realised. Mr Evans decided to send his daughter away from him and to vacate the house at Foleshill; Marian determined to take lodgings in Leamington and to support herself by teaching. Her brother Isaac, however, now married and living at Griff, persuaded her to stay with him and to hope for a change in their father's attitude. Around the same time, Mary Sibree's father, minister of an independent chapel, brought in outside help in order to 'bring forward the best arguments in favour of orthodox doctrines'. The first attempt ended unsuccessfully with the visiting authority (a Baptist minister) remarking:

'That young lady must have had the devil at her elbow to suggest her doubts, for there was not a book that I recommended to her in support of Christian evidences that she had not read'. A professor from a religious college in Birmingham fared no better: '*She* has gone into the question', he was heard to observe after an unsuccessful interview (Cross, i, 362). In the end, a compromise was reached. Marian agreed to resume attendance at church and her father allowed that she could hold whatever opinions she wished.

Loss of faith was unquestionably a change for the better in Marian's life. She writes to one correspondent of her inexpressible relief in being freed from the apprehension 'that at each moment I tread on chords that will vibrate for weal or woe to all eternity' and that she could shed tears of joy because she can now lie on the ground and ruminate without dreading 'lest my conclusions should be everlastingly fatal' (*L*, i, 143–4). Once she no longer ranked among her principles of action 'a fear of vengeance eternal, gratitude for predestined salvation, or a revelation of future glories as a reward', she was able to turn her attention towards this world and to 'the duty of *finding* happiness' (*L*, i, 125, 133).

Because of its eudemonistic flavour, however, the above quotation is unrepresentative of all but the initial phase of Marian's freedom from dogmatic belief. More characteristic of her thinking and her sensibility from first to last is the letter describing her religious views that she wrote to Sara Hennell in October 1843 – an impressively mature and penetrating statement for a provincial young woman of twenty-three who only two years before had remained racked and stretched on a 'wretched giant's bed of dogmas'. When first liberated from this confinement, 'there is a feeling of exaltation and strong hope' that we shall soon 'obtain something positive' both to compensate for what was previously renounced and to offer to others:

But a year or two of reflection and the experience of our own miserable weakness which will ill afford to part even with the crutches of superstition must, I think, effect a change. Speculative truth begins to appear but a shadow of individual minds, agreement between intellects seems unattainable, and we turn to the *truth of feeling* as the only universal bond of union. We find that the intellectual errors which we once fancied were a mere incrustation have grown into the living body and that we cannot in the majority of causes, wrench them away without destroying vitality. We begin to find with individuals, as with nations, the only safe revolution is one arising out of the wants which their *own progress* has generated.

(*L*, i, 162).

In the absence of something of her own to offer to others, Marian devoted herself during the mid 1840s to translating into English Strauss' *Life of Jesus*, a magnum opus of German biblical criticism. In contrast to Hennell's commonsense empirical approach to the Christian legends, Strauss' work exemplified the philosophic spirit characteristic of the Germans. He was unsatisfied with both super-natural explanations of the Gospels and the naturalistic explana-tions of the rationalists, preferring a new 'mythical mode of interpretation' which relinquished 'the historical reality of the sacred narratives in order to preserve to them an absolute inherent truth'. This truth – 'the dogmatic import of the life of Jesus' – was the subject of his 'Concluding Dissertation'. The foregoing 700 pages of historical inquiry, wrote Strauss, had 'annihilated', 'up-rooted', and 'withered' all the traditional Christian beliefs and consolations. Man now seemed divested of his dignity and the tie between heaven and earth broken. But what had been taken away with the hand of historical inquiry was now given back with the hand of dogma as it became clear that the philosophic spirit underlying Strauss' work was Hegelian. History was the story of the development of spirit and its progress through various histori-cal manifestations to an ultimate unity. The 'idea of the unity of the divine and human natures' made 'a far higher sense' when the whole race of mankind rather than a single man in past time was regarded as its ultimate realisation. The key to Christology was to replace the individual with 'the idea of the race . . . Humanity is the union of the two natures – God become man, the infinite manifesting itself in the finite, and the finite spirit remembering its infinitude'. Thus, 'the object of faith is completely changed: in-stead of a sensible, empirical fact, it has become a spiritual and divine idea, which has its confirmation no longer in history but in philosophy'.[5]

Marian laboured for almost two years on her translation of the almost half a million words of the *Life*, which was finally published in 1846. She was later to speak of translators as 'brokers in the great intellectual traffic of the world' (*Leader*, 9 February 1856, 140) and she no doubt derived a certain satisfaction from participating in this circulation from her study at Foleshill. But the work itself was wearying, a 'soul-stupefying labour' to which she ceased to sit down with any relish long before it was finished (*L*, i, 185). This will not surprise anyone who has attempted to read through her translation, which is as unrelievedly ponderous as Hennell's *Inquiry* is comparatively crisp. At one point while working on the *Life*, Marian vowed that she would never translate again. But in the late 1840s she undertook a translation of the Latin of Spinoza's *Tractatus Theologico-Politicus*, a seventeenth-century forerunner of nineteenth-century biblical criticism, which she must have found much more temperamentally congenial than the cerebral and philosophic cast of Strauss' new Christology because of Spinoza's emphasis on the fundamental importance in religious experience not of ideas but of universal moral laws that are inscribed in the heart.

In the same year that she began work on Spinoza, Marian wrote her first review of a novel. Published in the Coventry *Herald and Examiner* in March 1849, it was an encomium of James Anthony Froude's *The Nemesis of Faith*, which was described as one of those books that 'carry magic in them [and] are the true products of genius'.[6] The novel concerns an Oxford undergraduate whose preparations for Anglican ordination are complicated by doubts centring on the vengeful God of the Old Testament. After much inward struggle, the young man takes orders but resolves to give only ethical, not religious instruction. But he is eventually forced to give up his living; the last part of the novel finds him in Italy in love with a married woman, consumed with remorse when her child dies of a fever, saved from suicide by an English Roman Catholic priest, and dying in a monastery with his faith still unsettled.

The subject of *The Nemesis of Faith* – the crisis of belief and the loss of faith – is one of the great topoi of Victorian literature and the acute degree of destabilisation suffered by the doubter is typical of the literary texts dealing with the subject. Like the other young Hegelians in Germany, Strauss had 'passed from belief to unbelief gradually, without a crisis, without agony'.[7] But just the opposite was the case with most Victorian doubters, of whom the prototype is Carlyle, who presented a slightly fictionalised description of his unconversion in the second book of *Sartor Resartus* (1833–34). The nadir is reached in 'The Everlasting No' chapter, in which heaven and earth seem to the protagonist 'but boundless Jaws of a devouring Monster, wherein I, palpitating, waited to be devoured'.

Marian's extravagant praise of Froude's turgid and confused novel looks very much a personal estimate by someone who had herself undergone a passage from belief to non-belief. But what is most striking in comparing her unconversion not only to that of Froude's protagonist but also to those of other Victorian doubters is that it was accomplished without protracted inward agony. One reason is that Marian's passage from belief to unbelief was mediated by the high intellectual seriousness of Charles Hennell and by her own emergent belief in the powers and the beneficent progressive tendency of the intellect. In *Sartor Resartus* and Tennyson's *In Memoriam*, the intellectual powers of the mind are presented as being of inferior status: 'Not our Logical, Mensurative faculty, but our Imaginative one is King over us', says Carlyle's protagonist; Knowledge is 'half-grown as yet, a child, and vain', says Tennyson, and needs the guiding hand of Wisdom that is 'heavenly of the soul'; and he contrasts 'the freezing reason's colder part' to 'a warmth within the breast' that brings supernatural reassurance. Marian Evans, on the other hand, was committed to intellectual inquiry (even if speculative truth seemed unattainable). If properly pursued, such inquiry resulted in 'an expansion of one's own being' and led to the acquisition of 'the flexibility, the ready sympathy, [and] the tolerance which characterizes a truly philosophic culture'. For her:

> The spirit which doubts the ultimately beneficial tendency of inquiry, which thinks that morality and religion will not bear the broadest daylight our intellect can throw on them, though it may clothe itself in robes of sanctity and use pious phrases, is the worst form of atheism; while he who believes, whatever else he may deny, that the true and the good are synonymous, bears in his soul the essential element of religion.
>
> (*Essays*, 28, 42)

Another key difference between Marian and her doubting contemporaries is intimated in the above quotation: her assurance that moral values are not dependent on supernatural belief. Froude's protagonist loses his sense of morality when he loses his faith; and Carlyle and Tennyson both insisted that moral sanctions and a sense of human worth were wholly dependent on transcendental intuitions. Marian, on the other hand, assured the professor from Birmingham who had unsuccessfully tried to reconvert her that, while it was 'no small sacrifice to part with the assurance' of immortality, she did not believe 'the conviction that immortality is man's destiny indispensable to the production of elevated and heroic virtue and the sublimest resignation' (*L*, i, 136).

The assurance was rooted not only in Marian's belief in the beneficent tendency of intellectual inquiry but also in the '*truth of feeling*' and in her sense of the supreme value of human love. There is a strong autobiographical cast to the story of Maggie Tulliver in *The Mill on the Floss*, but the story has nothing to do with questions of supernatural belief. It rather concerns the need for love which is Maggie's leitmotif throughout the novel. For Marian Evans, as she wrote in 1855, the highest tendency of the Victorian age, with which she was fully in sympathy, was the sanctification of human love as a religion. This tendency was apparent even in *In Memoriam*: in a most perceptive comment, she noted that whatever the 'immediate prompting' of Tennyson's poem, 'whatever the form under which the author represented his aim to himself', the poem's deepest significance had to do with the supreme value attached, not to divine, but to human love (*WR*, 64 [1855], 597).

Let us return to the subject of the inner life of Marian Evans during her formative years, particularly her need for human love. In later years, she would say of the story of Maggie Tulliver, which details the oppressive narrowness of her lot, that her own experience was much worse and that in the novel 'everything [was] softened, as compared with real life' (*L*, viii, 465). And she told John Walter Cross that if she were to write an autobiography, 'the only thing I should much care to dwell on would be the absolute despair I suffered from of ever being able to achieve anything. No one could ever have felt greater despair' (Cross, i, 27).

In understanding Marian's inner life during her years at Foleshill, it is essential to realise that the longings, introspective habits, and emotional intensities that characterised her evangelical adolescence did not vanish after she shed her religious beliefs. One abiding inner quality was the habit of severe self-scrutiny. Herbert Spencer, who knew her intimately during the early 1850s, noted that Marian constantly studied her own defects. She complained to him of being 'troubled by double consciousness – a current of self-criticism being an habitual accompaniment of anything she

was saying or doing; and this naturally tended towards self-
depreciation and self-distrust'.[8] Another lasting quality was an
intensity of aspiration and the desire to be wholly consumed in
something beyond self. She recognised this 'ever struggling ambition' as her besetting sin; and was apprehensive lest her 'increased
uncertainty' concerning her future become so intense as to 'un-
hinge my mind a little' (*L*, i, 73).

But Marian's greatest source of anxiety concerned her need to be
loved – to find an answering other to satisfy the longings of an
intensely emotional nature. A classmate at the Miss Franklins'
school recalled noticing in Marian's German dictionary some evi-
dently original verses expressing a need for love and sympathy.
The same sentiment is repeatedly expressed in letters written
during her late 'teens and early twenties: 'I begin to feel involun-
tarily isolated, and without being humble, to have . . . a consciousness that I am a negation of all that finds love and esteem';
'the voice of foreboding . . . has long been telling me, "The bliss of
reciprocated affection is not allotted to you under any form"'; 'I am
alone in the world . . . I mean that I have no one who enters into
my pleasure or my griefs, no one with whom I can pour out my
soul' (*L*, i, 51, 70, 102). There is no doubt that the specific object of
Marian's longing was for a man to love her and that the reciprocated affection she craved could not be supplied by someone of her
own sex. As she explained in the last year of her life to Edith
Simcox, her too passionate admirer: 'the love of men and women
for each other must always be more and better than any other'; the
'friendship and intimacy of men' had always meant more to her
than female relationships (*L*, ix, 299).

Isaac Evans thought that his sister's chances of finding a mate
had not improved after the move to Foleshill even though this had
been a principal reason for the relocation, and that her renunciation of Christianity had made matters worse. In the brother's view,
Marian had 'no chance of getting the one thing needful – i.e. a
husband and a settlement, unless she mixes more in society'. But
her shyness and intellectual seriousness did not facilitate conventional social intercourse. Moreover, since she had come to know
the Brays she seldom went anywhere else; in Isaac's view, Charles
Bray, 'being only a leader of mobs, can only introduce her to
Chartists and Radicals, and that such only will ever fall in love with
her if she does not belong to the Church' (*L*, i, 156–7). Marian did
receive one offer of marriage during the 1840s. It came from a

young artist and/or picture restorer from Leamington who despite being poor hoped to be able to support a wife. But this was hardly the kind of offer Isaac had in mind; in any event, having detected signs of mental instability in her suitor, Marian had already decided to end their relationship before the proposal was made (see *L*, ix, 336–7).

Another complicating factor in Marian's longing for love was her physical unattractiveness, for which there is ample pictorial and written evidence. When Sofia Kovalevskaya first met her in 1869, she was shocked by Marian's appearance: 'A small, thin little figure, with a heavy head which seemed too large in proportion; the mouth with huge, protruding 'English' teeth; the nose, although straight and beautiful in outline, was too prominent for a female face . . . a black dress of light, half transparent material . . . betrayed the thinness of her neck and emphasised the sickly yellowness of her face'.[9] And in the same year Henry James made similar observations after his first meeting: 'she is magnificently ugly', James wrote to his father, 'deliciously hideous. She has a low forehead, a dull grey eye, a vast pendulous nose, a huge mouth, full of uneven teeth, and a chin and jaw-bone *qui n'en finissent pas*' (Haight, 417). But the most telling evidence is supplied by the subject, who clearly considered herself to be ugly and made numerous references to the fact in her correspondence. Some of these references were humourous, but Marian's physical unattractiveness was not always a laughing matter, certainly not when she was in her early thirties and a man to whom she had become passionately attached cited her lack of physical beauty as a reason he could not respond to her love.

But that was in the 1850s. In the late 1830s and 1840s, there was one man in her life to whom she was deeply attached and from whom she professed no wish to be separated: her father Robert Evans. The narrator of *The Mill on the Floss* speaks of the 'sense of oppressive narrowness [that] has acted on young natures in many generations, that in the outward tendency of human things have risen above the mental level of the generation before them, to which they have been nevertheless tied by the strongest fibres of their hearts' (ch. 30). It is hard not to think that this same sense pressed on Marian's consciousness during the long years from mid-adolescence to her thirtieth year when she lived with and cared for her father. But there can be no doubt at all that she was tied to him by the strongest fibres of her heart. And it is equally clear from her letters that she did not wish her lot to be other than what it was. 'I have the greatest of satisfactions to my mind', she wrote in 1842, 'in witnessing and perhaps slightly administering to my father's comfort'; and three years later she reported to an old friend that 'I and father go on living and loving together as usual, and it is my chief source of happiness to know that I form one item of his' (L, i, 152, 189).

By the mid-1840s Robert Evans was in his seventies and his health was beginning to fail. During these years, Marian was able to make his evenings cheerful by reading Walter Scott's novels aloud to him. But as the father's health deteriorated, there was increasingly little that could be done to cheer him. In April of 1848 he was so ill that she resolved to sleep in his bedroom until he improved; she wrote to her sister that it had been a greater trial than she had ever had 'to see him suffering for so many weeks together'. In September Caroline Bray wrote to her sister that Marian's father 'gets rapidly worse. The doctors expect his death to take place suddenly, by a suffusion of water on the chest; and poor M.A., alone with him, has the whole care and fatigue of nursing him night and day with this constant nervous expectation. She keeps up wonderfully mentally, but looks like a ghost' (L, i, 258, 272).

During this period, Marian must have been experiencing the truth of feeling with an unprecedented intensity from which all sense of oppressiveness was excluded. As she was to observe in her first book:

> As we bend over the sick-bed, all the forces of our nature rush towards the channels of pity, of patience, and of love, and sweep down the miserable choking drift of our quarrels, our debates, our would-be wisdom, and our clamorous selfish desires. This blessing of serene freedom from the importunities of opinion lies in all simple direct acts of mercy, and is one source of that sweet calm which is often felt by the watcher in the sick-room, even when the duties there are of a hard and terrible kind.
>
> (*Janet's Repentance*, ch. 24)

The following May, when her father's death was at last imminent, Marian reflected that 'Strange to say I feel that these will ever be the happiest days of life to me. The one deep strong love I have ever known has now its highest exercise and fullest reward'. Robert Evans died on 31 May 1849. 'What shall I be without my Father?' Marian had asked on the eve of his death: 'It will seem as if a part of my moral nature were gone. I had a horrid vision of myself last night becoming earthly sensual and devilish for want of that pure restraining influence' (*L*, i, 283–4). Already in her thirtieth year, Marian was left to face the uncertain future with no one to love her and no idea of what to do with the remainder of her life.

2
London 1850–1857

She was of a most affectionate disposition, always requiring some one to lean upon . . . She was not fitted to stand alone.

Charles Bray

I do hope you will not bother your soul about what the Westminster says. The woman who used to insult you therein . . . is none other than Miss Evans, the infidel esprit forte, who is now G.H. Lewes' concubine.

Charles Kingsley to F.D. Maurice

Six days after her father's funeral, Marian left for the continent with the Brays. They returned to England the following month, but she stayed on in Geneva for the next eight months – living first in a pension on the lake and then as a lodger in the home of M. D'Albert and his family. While at the former, Marian entertained her correspondents back in England with descriptions of the other guests, including two American ladies who 'chatter the most execrable French with amazing volubility and self-complacency. They are very rich, very smart, and very vulgar'; and an Italian marquise who one day dressed Marian's hair for her in a new style which everyone said made her look 'infinitely better . . . though to myself I seem uglier than ever – if possible' (*L*, i, 290–1, 298). At the D'Albert's she had her own piano, participated in weekly musical parties, and made the acquaintance of a number of cultivated Genevans. But while she widened her social and cultural horizons, Marian's stay in Switzerland was essentially a time of loneliness and introspection during which, as she later recalled, her life 'seemed to serve no purpose of much worth' and she was 'very unhappy, and in a state of discord and rebellion towards my own lot' (*L*, iii, 187, 230–1).

The next few years were to be crucially determining ones for Marian and it is unfortunate that more cannot be known about her inner life during this period. She had begun to keep a journal while in Geneva, but either she or John Walter Cross, her widower and biographer, destroyed its first forty-six pages, covering the years from 1849 to 1854. And with few exceptions, Marian no longer used her letters for introspective or confessional purposes (as she had in her letters to Maria Lewis). There can be no doubt, however, that a large part of her unhappiness and anxiety during this period related to the problem of vocation – to her having 'no purpose of much worth'. In *Sartor Resartus*, Carlyle had defined the problem with which many gifted individuals were to grapple during the nineteenth century: 'To each is given a certain inward Talent, a certain outward Environment of Fortune; to each, by wisest combination of these two, a certain maximum of Capability. But the hardest problem were ever this first: To find by study of yourself, and of the ground you stand on, what your combined inward and outward Capability specially is'. Marian was not back in England long before she was observing: 'We are apt to complain of the weight of duty, but when it is taken from us, and we are left at liberty to choose for ourselves, we find that the old life was the easier one'. And in another letter she exhorted a correspondent in distinctly Carlylean tones to remember 'but two words of very vital significance for you and me and all mortals – *Resignation* and labour' (*L*, i, 334, 359).

But what labour for Marian Evans? She could not live on the income of £90 per annum that the interest on the sum left her by her father provided; and she was determined not to be dependent on her siblings, especially since her sister Chrissey, with six children and a bankrupt husband, was much more in need of help. Virtually the only career open to an educated woman at the time was teaching – either in a school or as a governess in a private family. Neither prospect was at all appealing. A possible alternative was for the translator of Strauss to attempt to earn a living with her pen. An opportunity to explore this possibility came in October 1850, while Marian was staying with the Brays. John Chapman, the London publisher, came to visit accompanied by one of his authors, R.W. Mackay, whose *Progress of the Intellect, as Exemplified in the Religious Development of the Greeks and Hebrews* had recently been published. It was agreed that Marian would review the book for Chapman's new acquisition, the *Westminster Review*. When she brought the finished review to London in November she stayed for two weeks in Chapman's house at 142 Strand in one of the second floor rooms he rented. By the end of her stay she had resolved to return – to live in London and to look for literary work to support herself.

In January 1851 Marian wrote from 142 Strand to Mary Sibree, assuring her that she had not lost her old sympathies 'though I am among new people and very much occupied with egotistic thoughts and feelings' (*L*, i, 344). One may assume that, like Dorothea Brooke in *Middlemarch*, her thoughts were egotistical in having as their focus a 'tumultuous preoccupation with her personal lot' (ch. 20). And given the humiliating events that took place in Chapman's house during the early months of 1851, it seems clear that the egotism of Marian's feelings also involved the need to love and to have someone to lean on. What transpired during this period is known mainly through the journal of Chapman, who was twenty-nine, handsome, and a womaniser. He lived with a wife fourteen years his senior and their three young children, who were looked after by Elizabeth Tilley, a good-looking woman of thirty who was also Chapman's mistress. A liaison of some degree of intimacy, 'probably more serious than holding hands', as her biographer puts it (Haight, 86), developed between Chapman and Marian. She was unaware of the dual role played in the Chapman ménage by Miss Tilley, who noticed the intimacy, became jealous, and conspired with Chapman's wife to drive Marian from the house. When she left to return to Coventry, Chapman accompanied her to the railway. 'She was very sad . . . She pressed me for some intimation of the state of my feelings, – I told her that I felt great affection for her, but that I loved E. and S. also, though each in a different way. At this avowal she burst into tears. I tried to comfort her, and reminded [her] of the dear friends and pleasant home she was returning to, – but the train whirled her away very very sad' (Haight, 85–6).

It is clear that Marian had fallen in love with Chapman, and that she was still deeply attached to him the following October when she agreed to return to live at 142 Strand and serve without pay as the de facto managing editor of the *Westminster Review*. This journal of radical opinion had been started by the Benthamites and its former editors included John Stuart Mill. But by the time it came into Chapman's hands, the journal had lost its cutting edge. The new owner was determined to restore its sharpness as 'the bold and uncompromising exponent of the most advanced and philosophical views in reference to the various subjects it will discuss' (*L*, viii, 38). Marian lived and worked at Chapman's house from the fall of 1851 to October 1853 and continued as editor until July of the following year. Her duties were heavy. She advised on the choice of authors and subjects, commissioned articles, corresponded with the contributors, copy-edited the manuscripts making the necessary cuts and rearrangements, did all the proofreading, and saw each issue through the press. In addition, in order to supplement her meagre income, she planned to write a book on the idea of a future life, took on the job of translating Feuerbach's *Essence of Christianity*, and made plans to write articles and reviews of her own. At times she expressed dissatisfaction with the amount of her work and the conditions of her employment, more than once having to console herself with the thought that 'the Review would be a great deal worse if I were not here' (*L*, ii, 88). But on the whole, life at 142 Strand during these years was clearly good for Marian. She was able to take advantage of the cultural life of London – the concerts, the theatre, the exhibitions of paintings; and the lively social life at Chapman's brought her into contact with liberal intellectuals, Utilitarians, women's rights activists, scientists, historians, philosophers, religious thinkers and men of letters. And her editorial position made her a much more important participant in the intellectual traffic of the world than she had been as a provincial translator. The contributors to *Westminster Review* could write more openly in its pages than anywhere else. 'They are amongst the world's vanguard', she declared: 'it is good for the world, therefore, that they should have every facility for speaking out' (*L*, ii, 49); and Marian Evans, who brought author and subject together, was the principal facilitator. Thomas Henry Huxley agreed to review scientific books; Mazzini was asked to write on freedom vs. despotism; Charlotte Brontë might be asked for an article on modern novelists; G.H. Lewes could write on Lamarck's evolutionary theories; Harriet Martineau did a piece on 'The Condition and Prospects of Ireland'; J.A. Froude wrote on the Oxford Commission, Herbert Spencer on 'The Philosophy of Style', James Martineau on 'The Restoration of Belief'; and so on through the quarterly cycles of planning, improvisation, disappointment and 'hope that our next number will be the best yet' (*L*, ii, 33–4).

Through her association with the review, Marian also made new friendships with persons responsive to her unusual qualities. Two of them were Bessie Parkes and Barbara Leigh Smith (later Bodichon). Both were young women of advanced views who were involved in the women's rights movement. The former was to become editor of the *English Women's Journal*, which advocated education and employment for women; the latter helped start the campaign for women's suffrage and was one of the group who founded Girton College. It was to Barbara that Bessie wrote the following about their new friend: 'The odd mixture of truth and fondness in Marian is so great. She never spares, but expresses every opinion, good and bad, with the most unflinching plainness, and yet she seems able to see faults without losing tenderness' (*L*, ii, 87). Another person who became a close friend was the philosopher Herbert Spencer, whose *Social Statics* had come out in 1850 and who was a frequent contributor to the *Westminster*, in which he was publishing sketches of the doctrines later elaborated in his *Principles of Psychology* and other books. Soon after meeting her, Spencer was writing to a friend that Miss Evans was 'the most admirable woman, mentally, I ever met', and that he went very frequently to Chapman's where 'the greatness of her intellect, conjoined with her womanly qualities and manner, generally keep me by her side most of the evening'.[1] And although he never became an intimate friend, William Hale White (Mark Rutherford), who also lodged at 142 Strand during the early 1850s, was equally drawn to Marian. 'She never reserved herself', White remembered, 'but always said what was best in her at the moment, even when no special demand was made upon her. Consequently, she found out what was best in everybody'.[2]

Marian's letters during this period show a distinct sense of relief at the distance that now lay between herself and her family. 'I am delighted', she wrote as early as 1850, 'to feel that I am of no importance to any of them, and have no motive for living amongst them' (*L*, i, 336). In London, Marian had a room of her own, admiring friends, and something worthwhile at which to labour. For anyone unaware of the ruling passion of her inner life – the need for someone to lean on – she might have been thought to be happy. But the question she had asked on the eve of her father's death – what she would do without his 'pure restraining influence' – remained unanswered. Indeed, the disastrous intimacy with Chapman had suggested that she was not fully in control of her emotions and that her need for love could become a destructive force in her life. And then, only a little over a year after the jealousy of Chapman's mistress had forced her to return to Coventry, a similar episode occurred, this time involving Herbert Spencer.

In April 1852 she and Spencer were engaging in playful badinage; in the late spring and early summer they were enjoying frequent conversations during long walks together, and rumours concerning their engagement had even begun to circulate. Spencer began to be concerned about their constant companionship: while he greatly admired Marian intellectually, he could not sense in himself 'any indications of a warmer feeling'. He wrote to her indicating his concerns and then, realising that he had presumed the likelihood of feelings on her part that might not in fact exist, wrote a second time apologising for the first letter. Marian seemed to take it all 'smilingly' and their intimacy continued as before. But then, Spencer recalled, 'just that which I had feared might take place, did take place. Her feelings became involved and mine did not. The lack of physical attraction was fatal'. In July, Marian wrote to Spencer the most pathetic and wrenching of all the letters in the nine volumes of her collected correspondence:

I want to know if you can assure me that you will not forsake me, that you will always be with me as much as you can and share your thoughts and feelings with me. If you become attached to someone else, then I must die, but until then I could gather courage to work and make life valuable, if only I had you near me. I do not ask you to sacrifice anything – I would be very good and cheerful and never annoy you. But I find it impossible to contemplate life under any other conditions. If I had your assurance, I could trust that and live upon it. I have struggled – indeed I have – to renounce everything and be utterly unselfish, but I find myself utterly unequal to it. Those who have known me best have always said, that if ever I loved anyone thoroughly my whole life must turn upon that feeling, and I find they said truly. You curse the destiny which has made the feeling concentrate itself on you – but if you will only have patience with me you shall not curse it long. You will find that I can be satisfied with very little, if I am delivered from the dread of losing it.

I suppose no woman ever before wrote such a letter as this – but I am not ashamed of it, for I am conscious that in the light of reason and true refinement I am worthy of your respect and tenderness, whatever gross men or vulgar-minded women might think of me.

(L, viii, 42–3, 56–7)

It was, as Spencer recalled, 'a most painful affair,' which continued without resolution through the autumn of 1852 and into the new year: 'She was very desponding and I passed the most miserable time that has occurred in my experience; for, hopeless as the relation was, she would not agree that we should cease to see one another' (L, viii, 43). The situation only began to improve when Spencer met an acquaintance one afternoon while on his way to visit Marian and invited him to come along. The acquaintance was George Henry Lewes (pronounced Lewis), co-editor of the *Leader*, a progressive weekly. The two men visited Marian several more times until one day, when Spencer rose to leave, Lewes said he would stay. By March he had become a regular visitor and had 'quite won my liking, in spite of myself' (L, ii, 94). Their relationship deepened during the following months and in October 1853 Marian moved out of Chapman's house into lodgings of her own. According to Gordon Haight, it was at this time that their physical intimacy began.

George Henry Lewes had been born in London in 1817 and been at school in Brittany and Jersey, as well as in England. During his early twenties he had spent much time in Germany and had subsequently tried and abandoned careers in commerce and medicine; and his intermittent interest in professional acting continued until 1849. When Marian came to know him, he had been earning his living by his pen for some time. The four volumes of a *Biographical History of Philosophy* had come out in the 1840s, as had a book on the Spanish drama. They had been followed by two novels and then in 1849 by a life of Robespierre, which the revolutionary upheavals of the previous year had prompted him to prepare. But the bulk of his writing was done for one or another of the quarterlies and other reviews that were a prominent feature of the intellectual life of Victorian Britain. This work included a good deal of literary and dramatic criticism; but there were few subjects on which Lewes was unable to supply an article, and by the time Marian came to know him he had established himself as one of the most prolific and versatile journalists in London.

John Stuart Mill did not think that Lewes was a coxcomb, but thought he was 'very likely to be thought so'. Jane Carlyle had a not dissimilar view. She described 'little Lewes' as 'the most amusing little fellow in the whole world – if you only look over his unparalleled *impudence* which is not impudence at all but man-of-genius-*bonhomie* . . . He is [the] best mimic in the world and full of famous stories, and no spleen or envy, or *bad* thing in him, so see that you receive him with open arms in spite of his immense ugliness'.[3] There is a good deal of other contemporary reference to the ugliness of Lewes, whose face showed the ravages of smallpox; but even when she first knew him, Marian seems not to have been bothered by either his appearance or his impudent-seeming manner; 'a sort of miniature Mirabeau in appearance' was her only comment on first meeting him in 1851. And in the spring of 1853 she assured Caroline Bray that, 'like a few other people in the world, he is much better than he seems . . . a man of heart and conscience wearing a mask of flippancy' (*L*, i, 367; ii, 98).

What did concern Marian as her intimacy with Lewes deepened was the fact that he had a wife and three young children. Lewes had married Agnes Jervis in 1841, when she was nineteen and he twenty-three; they had both held the same advanced views on social relations, including those between the sexes, and seem in other ways to have been perfectly compatible during the early years of their marriage. But by 1849 all was not well. As Jane Carlyle noted: 'I used to think these Leweses a perfect pair of love-birds always cuddling together on the same perch – to speak figuratively – but the female love-bird appears to have hopped off to some distance and to be now taking a somewhat critical view of her little shaggy mate!'[4] Agnes had in fact begun sleeping with Thornton Hunt, co-editor with Lewes of the *Leader*; in 1850, when she gave birth to another child, it was generally acknowledged to be Hunt's. Lewes was understanding; there were no recriminations and he had the child registered in his name. But the marriage continued to deteriorate and even before Agnes gave birth to a second child of Hunt's it was clear that her life with Lewes was over. Divorce was not a possibility even if Lewes had had the financial resources: having previously condoned his wife's adultery by giving her illegitimate child his name, he was thereafter precluded from seeking a legal dissolution of the union. Thus, by the time he became Marian's lover, Lewes' marriage had ended in all but the legal sense – though he continued, as he would until the end of his life, to contribute to the support of Agnes and her illegitimate children.

It was not until the summer of 1854 that Marian took the irrevocable decision to live openly with Lewes. That July they left together for Germany where they stayed until the end of the following winter. As news of their concubinage spread, Marian wrote to a few of her friends, not to defend her position, but to explain the facts of the case. She assured Charles Bray that Lewes had not '"run away" from his wife and family' and advised him to believe nothing 'beyond the simple fact that I am attached to him and that I am living with him' (*L*, ii, 178–9). And to Chapman, who had asked what reply to give to inquiries, she said in effect that it was nobody's business what she did: 'About my own justification I am entirely indifferent . . . I have done nothing with which any person has a right to interfere' (*L*, viii, 123–4). But to Caroline Bray, who had been deeply upset by her friend's open defiance of convention, Marian eventually did try to explain herself:

> if there be any one subject on which I feel no levity it is that of marriage and the relation of the sexes – if there is any one action or relation of my life which is and always has been profoundly serious, it is my relation to Mr. Lewes . . . one thing I can tell you in few words. Light and easily broken ties are what I neither desire theoretically nor could live for practically. Women who are satisfied with such ties do *not* act as I have done – they obtain what they desire and are still invited to dinner.
>
> . . . From the majority of persons, of course, we never looked for anything but condemnation. We are leading no life of self-indulgence, except indeed, that being happy in each other, we find everything easy. We are working hard to provide for others better than we provide for ourselves, and to fulfil every responsibility that lies upon us.
>
> (*L*, ii, 213–14)

Marian was not wrong in anticipating condemnation of her action. Even the free-thinking Chapman was concerned with the social consequences: 'Now, I can only pray, against hope, that he may prove constant to her; otherwise she is *utterly* lost' (*L*, viii, 126). George Combe, the Edinburgh phrenologist and supporter of the *Westminster*, who was a friend and admirer of Marian's, was completely unsympathetic:

> 'The greatest happiness of the greatest number' principle, appears to me to require that the obligations of married life should be honourably fulfilled; and an educated woman who, in the face of the world, volunteers to live as a wife, with a man who already has a living wife and children, appears to me to pursue a course and to set an example calculated only to degrade herself and her sex, if she be sane. – If you receive her into your family

circle, while present appearances are unexplained, pray consider whether you will do justice to your own female domestic circle, and how other ladies may feel about going into a circle which makes no distinction between those who act thus, and those who preserve their honour unspotted?

(*L*, viii, 129–30)

It is not surprising that Marian put off telling her family about her relationship with Lewes for as long as she could. It was only in 1857 that she wrote to her brother to say that 'I have changed my name, and have someone to take care of me in the world. The event is not at all a sudden one . . . My husband has been known to me for several years . . .' Isaac Evans was furious at not having been consulted as to his sister's intentions and prospects, and gave her letter to his solicitor to answer. It was only in reply to the lawyer's letter that Marian revealed that 'Our marriage is not a legal one, though it is regarded by us both as a sacred bond . . . I have been his wife and have borne his name for nearly three years' (*L*, ii, 331, 349). Isaac's response was to break off all communication with Marian and to insist that his siblings do the same. It was not until twenty-two years later, on the occasion of her legal marriage to John Walter Cross, that he again communicated with her.

Marian's union with Lewes brought her great personal happiness. She was scarcely exaggerating when she wrote from Germany in August 1854 that she seemed to have begun life afresh. One may assume that part of this freshness was sexual; there is no reason to doubt the conjecture of her biographer that 'at thirty-four her deeply passionate nature had at last found a wholly satisfying love that responded keenly to Lewes's more experienced sexuality' (Haight, 145). There were to be no children from this union: Barbara Leigh Smith reported to Bessie Parkes that the couple practised some form of contraception and did not intend to start a family. Their only offspring, so to speak, were to be the George Eliot novels; as we shall see, her happy and fulfilled life with Lewes was the enabling condition of the belated germination of her creative powers. But there is first an intervening stage of Marian's career to be considered, the trigger of which was not her happiness with Lewes but the couple's financial difficulties.

In the mid-1850s, Lewes was earning around £400 a year, of which at least £250 went to Agnes and her household; and Marian had for some years been living on a shoestring. In their first years together, Lewes later recalled, 'we were very poor, living in one room, where I had my little table . . . and my wife another close at hand where she wrote' (Haight, 218). One of the projects at which Marian laboured was a translation of Spinoza's *Ethics*; but this proved completely unremunerative. She fared better with the copious periodical writing she now undertook. Between 1854 and 1856 she produced over thirty reviews and short articles for the *Leader*, seven 'Belles Lettres' review essays for the *Westminster*, in which a total of 166 books were noticed, and a number of substantial articles and review essays on a variety of subjects. There is a certain amount of pot-boiling going on in this body of writing; it is most apparent in the places where Marian is content to be descriptive, topical, and/or entertaining. But there is also ample evidence not only of her erudition but also of her even more impressive intelligence. These essays contain discursive formulations of the fundamental beliefs that inform her fiction. Before examining them, however, we must first consider her translation of Feuerbach's *Essence of Christianity*, which was published in 1854.

Like David Friedrich Strauss, his junior by four years, Ludwig Feuerbach belonged to the group of Young Hegelians. His *Wesen des Christenhums* (*Essence of Christianity*) was published at the beginning of the 1840s and had a great impact in Germany during that decade. As Friedrich Engels recalled: 'One must himself have experienced the liberating effect of this book to get an idea of it. Enthusiasm was general. We all became at once Feuerbachians'. The book was liberating because it had broken through the contradiction in Hegelian thought between the primacy of idea and the distinctiveness of nature and 'placed materialism on the throne again. Nature exists independently of all philosophy . . . Nothing exists outside nature and man, and the higher beings our religious fantasies have created are only the fantastic reflection of our own essence'. Hegelian notions of absolute idea and the pre-existence of logical categories before the world came into being were similarly revealed as 'nothing more than the fantastic survival of the belief in the existence of an extra-mundane creator'. Matter was not a product of the mind, but mind itself was 'merely the highest product of matter'.[5]

That was the effect of Feuerbach's book in general terms; more particularly, the *Essence of Christianity* was a frontal assault on the transcendental and supernatural postulates of traditional Christian belief. For Feuerbach, nothing transcended man. The true sense of theology was anthropology and that of metaphysics was psychology; there was 'no distinction between the *predicates*' of the divine and human subject. All the characteristic beliefs and symbols of the Christian religion could be thus newly interpreted to reveal their human meaning. The sacrament of baptism, for example, was truly significant only when it was regarded 'as a symbol of the value of water itself. Baptism should represent to us the wonderful but natural effect of water on man'. It did not have merely personal effects, 'but also, and as a result of these, moral and intellectual effects'. Water not only cleansed man of bodily impurities; 'in water the scales fall from his eyes: he sees, he thinks more clearly; he feels himself freer; water extinguishes the fire of appetite'.

The key to understanding the non-distinction of divine and human was Love – 'the middle term, the substantial bond, the principle of reconciliation between . . . the divine and the human. Love is God himself, and apart from it there is no God. Love makes man God and God man'. But in Christianity, 'love is tainted by faith . . . it needs not the sanction of faith; it is its own basis'. The love bounded by faith was 'a narrow-hearted, false love'. Indeed, 'all love founded on a special historical phenomenon contradicts the nature of love [which] should be immediate, undetermined by anything else than its object'. Marriage was the supreme example. All relations between human beings were *per se* religious. But 'marriage – we mean, of course, marriage as the free bond of love – is sacred in itself, by the very nature of the union which is therein effected'. A marriage, the bond of which was 'merely an external restriction, not the voluntary, contented self-restriction of love', was not a true or a 'truly moral' marriage.[6]

The above quotations are perhaps sufficient to give some idea of the constant rhetorical excesses and intermittent fatuities of Feuerbach's discourse. His English translator herself remarked that while 'with the ideas of Feuerbach I everywhere agree . . . of course I should, of myself, alter the phraseology considerably (*L*, ii, 153). It was not surprising that after a few years of notoriety, Feuerbach's reputation in Germany withered with startling speed; nor that in later years he became known as something of a crackpot because of his slogan that 'man is what he eats' and his assertion that the 1848 revolution failed in his country because potatoes rather than beans dominated the German diet. So complete was Feuerbach's eclipse that in his review in the *Westminster* of the translation by Marian Evans (it was to be the only time her real name appeared on a title page) James Martineau wondered why, 'if she wished to exhibit the new Hegelian Atheism to English readers, she should select a work . . . of quite secondary philosophical repute in its own country' (*L*, ii, 187).

The reason undoubtedly had much to do with the particular relevance of Feuerbach's views of love and marriage to Marian's situation during 1853 and 1854, as she was reaching the decision to live openly with Lewes in defiance of conventional morality. This pertinence, however, should not be allowed to obscure the distinction between the fine mind of Marian Evans and the comparatively crude mind of Feuerbach, and between her temperament and sensibility and his. Certainly the future author of the George Eliot novels believed deeply in a kind of religion of humanity and in the adequacy of human bonds as a replacement for superseded supernatural ones. As she wrote in an 1874 letter:

> my books . . . have for their main bearing a conclusion . . . without which I could not have cared to write any representation of human life – namely, that the fellowship between man and man which has been the principle of development, social and moral, is not dependent on conceptions of what is not man: and that the idea of God, so far as it has been a high spiritual influence, is the idea of a goodness entirely human (i.e., an exaltation of the human).
>
> (*L*, vi, 98)

It is equally true that from certain points of view – that of the Roman Catholic critic Richard Simpson, for example – her novels can seem programmatically Feuerbachian. For Simpson, 'the hidden meaning which lies under their plot, their dialogue, and their characters' was the atheistic theology of the Germans, 'the godless humanitarianism of Strauss and Feuerbach' (*CH*, 250, 225).

But in imaginative literature, temperament and sensibility are at least as important as ideas. Henry James once expressed his sense of 'the individual strong temperament in fiction' through the image of the projected light or 'color of the air' with which the 'painter of life . . . more or less unconsciously suffuses his picture'. This effect of atmosphere was distinct from subject matter or execution; it was not 'a matter of calculation and artistry', but rather an emanation of the 'spirit, temper, history' of the artist.

Why was it, James wondered about the work of one of the two or three novelists who meant most to him, 'that in George Eliot the sun sinks forever to the west, and the shadows are long, and the afternoon wanes, and the trees vaguely rustle, and the color of the day is much inclined to yellow'.[7] The reason, if one may presume to answer James, is that the touchstones of the temperament of Marian Evans are sorrow, sad experience and endurance. As her father lay dying, she had written that 'the worship of sorrow is *the* worship for mortals'. Nine years later, while still in the early phase of her happiness with Lewes and hard at work on her first novel, she reflected that 'people talk of the feelings dying out as one gets older – but at present my experience is just the contrary. All the serious relations of life become so much more real to one – pleasure seems so slight a thing, and sorrow and duty and endurance so great. I find the least bit of real human life touch me in a way it never did when I was younger' (*L*, i, 284; ii, 465).

That is why in the George Eliot novels there is no antagonism to traditional religious beliefs and practices, however much their adherents seem oblivious of the Feuerbachian dispensation. This crucial point is well illuminated in two passages from the novelist's letters. In 1859, writing to M. D'Albert, she spoke of the great changes that had been wrought in her in the decade since she lodged with him in Geneva:

> I no longer have any antagonism towards any faith in which human sorrow and human longing for purity have expressed themselves; on the contrary, I have a sympathy with it that predominates over all argumentative tendencies. I have not returned to dogmatic Christianity – to the acceptance of any set of doctrines as a creed, and a superhuman revelation of the Unseen – but I see in it the highest expression of the religious sentiment that has yet found its place in the history of mankind, and I have the profoundest interest in the inward life of sincere Christians in all ages.
>
> (*L*, iii, 231)

And in the following year she made this comment to Barbara Leigh Smith on the forms and ceremonies of Catholic worship:

> I feel no regret that any should turn to them for comfort, if they can find comfort in them: sympathetically, I enjoy them myself.

But I have faith in the working-out of higher possibilities than the Catholic or any other church has presented, and those who have strength to wait and endure, are bound to accept no formula which their whole souls – their intellect as well as their emotions – do not embrace with entire reverence. The highest 'calling and election' is to *do without opium* and live through all our pain with conscious, clear-eyed endurance.

(*L*, iii, 366)

Let us now turn to the essays of the mid-1850s. In them, Marian more than once reiterates her belief that, given the supersession of divine sanctions, human feeling alone can provide the foundation of morality. The view of the eighteenth-century poet Edward Young (it is identical with that of Tennyson in *In Memoriam*) was that 'Virtue with Immortality expires'. In her blistering attack on the author of *Night Thoughts*, Marian insisted that just the opposite was in fact the case. In so far as moral action is dependent on supernatural belief, the emotion that prompts the action 'is not truly moral – is still in the stage of egoism, and has not yet attained the higher development of sympathy'. The 'deep pathos lying in the thought of human mortality – that we are here for a little while and then vanish away, that this earthly life is all that is given to our loved ones and to our many suffering fellow-men – lies nearer the fountains of moral emotion than the conception of extended existence'. Even in the 'untheological minds' of plain people, this pathos could foster 'a delicate sense of our neighbour's rights, an active participation in the joys and sorrows of our fellow-men, [and] a magnanimous acceptance of privation or suffering . . . when it is the condition of good to others'. Moreover, as Marian insisted in a comparably scathing attack on the evangelical teaching of Dr Cumming, the substitution of a supernatural reference for 'the direct promptings of the sympathetic feelings' was a perversion more obstructive of moral development than anything else (*Essays*, 374–5, 187).

Both individual moral improvement and the moral progress of the race hinged on sympathy and fellow-feeling – the truth of which, as Marian had declared long before in her October 1843 letter to Sara Hennell, was 'the only universal bond of union'. Its antithesis was egotism, which in her fiction Marian sometimes seems to regard as a kind of original sin or primal taint to which is opposed the redeeming humanistic grace of fellow-feeling. It is the interaction, within individuals and between persons, of these opposing principles that is the core of the psychological and moral dramas enacted in the novels.

There are, however, certain necessary laws both within and without the individual that are crucial determinants of the play of these forces. As Marian noted in her 1851 review of Mackay's *Progress of the Intellect*, it was essential for human beings to recognise 'the presence of undeviating law in the material and moral world . . . that invariability of sequence which is acknowledged to be the basis of physical science, but which is still perversely ignored in our social organization, our ethics and our religion'. This 'inexorable law of consequences' (*Essays*, 31) is one of the most conspicuous thematic features of the George Eliot novels and poems. Nemesis and retribution are two of the terms used to describe its operation with reference to the individual moral life. The narrator of *Adam Bede* and its principal choric character are particularly insistent on the subject: 'Our deeds determine us, as much as we determine our deeds . . . There is a terrible coercion in our deeds'; 'apologetic ingenuity' after the fact may lead to a temporary period of 'placid adjustment', but this will inevitably be 'disturbed by a convulsive retribution'; 'Consequences are unpitying. Our deeds carry their terrible consequences . . . consequences that are hardly ever confined to ourselves' (chs. 29, 16). And in the novel's most rebarbative passage, it is said of the seventeen-year old Hetty Sorrell, who will come to grief as a result of her infatuation with the young squire, that she is 'spinning in young ignorance a light web of folly and vain hopes which may one day close round her and press upon her, a rancorous poisoned garment, changing all at once her fluttering trivial butterfly sensations into a life of deep human anguish' (ch. 22).

Adam Bede is not the only place in the George Eliot canon where the doctrine of consequences is so insistently promulgated, and so predictably shown in inexorable operation as to have a counterproductive effect on the reader and to suggest that Nemesis is not the working out of inner laws but the authorial introduction of a transcendent postulate to replace the Christian God and as such an example of the Victorian agnostic's desperate concern to maintain external moral sanctions. Certainly this is what Nietzsche thought in his comment on 'George Eliot' in *Twilight of the Idols*:

They are rid of the Christian God and now believe all the more firmly that they must cling to Christian morality. That is an English consistency; we do not wish to hold it against little moralistic females à la Eliot. In England one must rehabilitate oneself after every little emancipation from theology by showing in a veritably awe-inspiring manner what a moral fanatic one is. That is the penance they pay there.[8]

Marian's analysis of the inexorable laws *outside* the individual is less open to the charge of being factitious. As a social being, man was subject to forces that operated both diachronically and synchronically. These forces were the necessary laws of social development. The external conditions that society inherited from the past were not extrinsic to an individual but were the manifestations of inherited internal conditions in the human beings who composed the society. The external conditions and the internal related to each other as the organism to its medium, and individual development could take place 'only by the gradual consentaneous development of both'. The potentially tragic aspect of this interdependence was the subject of Sophocles' *Antigone*, which dramatised the conflict between two valid claims or principles. In Marian's analysis, the conflict between Antigone and Creon was a representation of the 'struggle between elemental tendencies and established laws' by which society ('the outer life of man') was 'gradually and painfully brought into harmony with [man's] inward needs' (*Essays*, 287, 264).

The key sustaining qualities for individuals who had attained a knowledge of 'the irreversible laws within and without' (as they are called in chapter 32 of *The Mill on the Floss*) were duty, resignation and renunciation. Human duty was 'comprised in the earnest study' of 'the inexorable law of consequences' and 'patient obedience to its teaching' (*Essays*, 31). A particular example was sketched by Marian in her 1868 'Notes on *The Spanish Gypsy*'. It was of a woman who has inherited a physical defect, a disease, or certain racial characteristics that make her repulsive to her community. In the face of such inherited misfortunes, it was almost a mockery to say to the woman 'Seek your own happiness'. The utmost approach to well-being that could be made in such a case was through 'large resignation and acceptance of the inevitable' (Cross, iii, 35). Renunciation, on the other hand, involved choice rather than acceptance. But the moral value and impressiveness of the act would be vitiated if there were a compensatory reward for

the choice. Such was the case in 'the copy-book morality' of a novel
Marian reviewed in 1855, which led her to insist:

> The notion that duty looks stern, but all the while has her hand
> full of sugar-plums, with which she will reward us by-and-by, is
> the favourite cant of optimists, who try to make out that this
> tangled wilderness of life has a plan as easy to trace as that of a
> Dutch garden; but it really undermines all true moral develop-
> ment by perpetually substituting something extrinsic as a motive
> to action, instead of the immediate impulse of love or justice,
> which alone makes an action truly moral.
>
> (*Essays*, 135)

In 1857 Marian Evans stopped criticising the fiction of others and
began writing her own. There was certainly a pecuniary aspect to
her doing so. For the periodical publication of her first story she
received 50 guineas, more than twice the sum Chapman had paid
for her long article on Edward Young, which had been by far the
more difficult to write. But the principal reason was that at the age
of thirty-seven, Marian had at last found her vocation. As late as
May 1854, after she had become a London literary intellectual and
found emotional fulfilment with Lewes, she had still spoken of
being afflicted by 'purely psychical' troubles – 'self-dissatisfaction
and despair of achieving anything worth the doing' (*L*, ii, 155–6).
But September 1856 marked the beginning of a 'new era in my life,
for it was then I began to write Fiction'.
   Marian had long had 'a vague dream . . . that some time or
other I might write a novel'. But she had never gone further than
an opening chapter describing a midlands village and the life of the
neighbouring farm houses; 'and as the years passed on I lost any
hope that I should ever be able to write a novel, just as I de-
sponded about everything else in my future life' (*L*, ii, 406). In the
early 1850s, Spencer had suggested she write fiction, but Marian
had lacked the self-confidence to heed his advice. It was not until
she had the encouragement of a man on whom she could lean that
her enormous creative powers began to stir. One morning, as she
lay in bed pondering what should be the subject of her first story,
her thoughts merged themselves into a 'dreamy doze' (*L*, ii, 407) –
a creative reverie similar to that which opens *The Mill on the Floss* –
during which she was borne back into her distant past: to the
church at Chilvers Coton and to the sad fortunes of the clergyman

whom she renamed Amos Barton. Once she had found her vocation, Marian's life seemed doubly blessed – both in the present and
prospectively. 'I am very happy', she wrote to Mary Sibree in 1857,

> happy in the highest blessing life can give us, the perfect love
> and sympathy of a nature that stimulates my own to healthful
> activity. I feel, too, that all the terrible pain I have gone through
> in past years partly from the defects of my own nature, partly
> from outward things, has probably been a preparation for some
> special work that I may do before I die. That is a blessed hope –
> to be rejoiced in with trembling.
>
> (*L*, ii, 343).

Her first novel, *Adam Bede*, published in 1859, was both a critical
and a popular success, and at this time her life with Lewes settled
into the pattern it would have until the latter's death in 1878.
Marian needed repeated encouragement and approbation in order
to persist in her 'special work'; she also needed to be sheltered
from the world. Lewes filled both roles; although he had time for
his own interests (which became increasingly scientific), his most
important occupation came to be the care and management of a
valuable literary property known to the reading public as George
Eliot. He gave Marian ideas and suggestions for her work, and
read or listened to her read her manuscripts as they were composed. He cheered her during frequent episodes of depression and
ill-health, and even when she was in good spirits was always ready
to help her to overcome the 'excessive diffidence' that would have
prevented her from writing 'if I were not beside her to encourage
her'. He was always alert to keep all criticism of her work from her.
'No one speaks about her books to her but me', he wrote in 1862;
'she sees no criticisms' (*L*, iv, 58). Lewes also transacted almost all
her business with her publishers and controlled access to her so
that she had 'the absolute necessity to me of an even, quiet life
when I am writing' (*L*, viii, 306). No wonder, then, that Marian
wrote on the manuscript of *The Legend of Jubal and Other Poems* that
she presented to him in 1874: 'To my beloved Husband, George
Henry Lewes, whose cherishing tenderness for twenty years has
alone made my work possible to me' (*L*, vi, 38).

As the years passed, the financial situation of Marian and Lewes
steadily improved. As early as 1863 Marian had acquired 'an
abundant independence', as she called it in her journal (Haight,

369). In 1873, owing to the success of *Middlemarch* and some shrewd investments, her income was almost £5000. Such sums allowed the couple to make frequent trips abroad as well as to provide for the education of Lewes' three sons. In 1863 they were able to buy the Priory, a comfortable home in St John's Wood not far from Regent's Park. It was there that they were visited one Sunday afternoon in January 1869 by Charles Eliot Norton, the American scholar and man of letters, who subsequently sent an account of the visit to an American friend. Norton had been received at the door by Lewes, who 'looks and moves like an old-fashioned French barber or dancing-master, very ugly, very vivacious, very entertaining'. Lunch was served in the study, the walls of which were covered with bookshelves, 'save over the fire-place where hung a staring likeness and odious vulgarizing portrait of Mrs Lewes'. Conversation with her 'was more than commonly interesting'; but her manner 'was too intense' and suggested that 'of a woman who feels herself to be of mark and is accustomed, as she is, to the adoring flattery of a coterie of not undistinguished admirers'.

Norton further reported that Marian was 'an object of great interest and great curiosity to society here'. Because of her irregular relationship with Lewes, she was 'not received in general society', and the women who visited her were 'either so émancipée as not to mind what the world says about them, or have no social position to maintain'. All in all, reported Norton, 'the common feeling is that it will not do for society to condone so flagrant a breach as hers of a convention and a sentiment (to use no stronger terms) on which morality greatly relies for support' (*L*, v, 7–9). Such had long been the social situation of Marian, who since her union with Lewes had lived 'cut off from what is called the world', accepting no invitations, returning no calls, and inviting only those who asked to visit her. Social disapproval gradually weakened during the 1870s as Marian's fame increased and social attitudes changed. But even if they had not, she would have had no reason to regret her decision to link her life openly with Lewes'. As Marian wrote to M. D'Albert in 1859: 'Under the influence of the intense happiness I have enjoyed in my married life from thorough moral and intellectual sympathy, I have at last found out my true vocation, after which my nature had always been feeling and striving uneasily without finding it . . . I have turned out to be an artist' (*L*, iii, 396, 186).

3
Critical Writings / *Scenes of Clerical Life* (1858)

> A very commonplace scene, indeed. But what scene was ever commonplace in the descending sunlight, when colour has awakened from its noonday sleep, and the long shadows awe us like a disclosed presence?
>
> *Janet's Repentance*

During adolescence, Marian Evans had read little prose fiction. The reasons are clear from a letter written to Maria Lewis in March 1839, the severe opinions of which closely resemble those of the Evangelical *Christian Observer*. Novels and romances were 'pernicious', and Marian feared she would carry 'to my grave the mental diseases with which they have contaminated me'. They had fed her dissatisfaction with the circumstances of her life and encouraged her to live in a fantasy world of her own creation, imagining scenes in which she was the chief actress. Any discipline one's mind received from fiction could be equally well supplied by history, which did not deal with 'things that never existed' (L, i, 22–3). In the last two decades of her life, after discovering her vocation, Marian once again developed an aversion to reading novels, though for a different reason. Whenever she was writing or only thinking of writing a novel, she could not risk reading any other English fiction because doing so blocked her creative flow. 'The other day', she wrote to her publisher in 1874, 'I did what I have sometimes done at intervals of five or six years – looked into three or four novels to see what the world was reading. The effect was paralyzing, and certainly justifies me in [my] abstinence from novel-reading' (L, vi, 75–6). But during the 1840s and 1850s, after she had shed her religious beliefs and before she became a professional novelist, Marian was an avid reader of novels. Until she began to review current fiction in the mid-1850s, however, she made relatively few written comments on her reading. These remarks need to be clustered and pointed up because her novel-reading during this period not only provided the comparative standards she would employ in her practical criticism; it also forms the long background of her own creative practise.

The most important novelist in Marian's reading experience was unquestionably Walter Scott, whom she began to read at the age of seven. During her Evangelical phase, his novels escaped proscription because they belonged to that class of 'standard works whose contents are matter of constant reference, and the names of whose heroes and heroines . . . conveniently describe characters and ideas' (*L*, i, 21). And later, 'when I was grown up and living alone with my Father, I was able to make the evenings cheerful for him during the last five or six years of his life by reading aloud to him Scott's novels. No other writer would serve as a substitute' (*L*, v, 175). In her periodical writing and her letters, one or another of Scott's novels or characters is frequently used as a standard of comparison or point of reference; and in 1855 Marian planned to make his novels the subject of an article. It is a great pity that she did not, for it would have allowed her to bring together and elaborate on a number of scattered observations: that Scott 'remains the unequalled model of historical romancists, however they may criticize him'; that he was 'full of historical and antiquarian knowledge; but . . . was pre-eminently a story-teller, an artist in fiction'; and that although Scott had 'the greatest combination of experience and faculty . . . he never made the most of his treasures, at least in his *mode* of presentation' (*WR*, 64 [1855], 290; 67 [1857], 323; *L*, iii, 378).

Other earlier English novelists whose work she knew well included Richardson and Jane Austen. The former was first read in 1847; previously Marian had had 'no idea that Richardson was worth so much'. The morality of *Sir Charles Grandison* was 'perfect – there is nothing for the new lights to correct' (*L*, i, 240). (She later said she was sorry that the novel was not even longer.) As for Jane Austen, in 1856 she was cited as one of the two standards of excellence for the genus of novels that depend for their interest 'on the delineation of quiet provincial life' (*WR*, 66 [1856], 262). And between February and June of the next year, while writing *Mr. Gilfil's Love Story*, the second of the *Scenes of Clerical Life*, Marian reread all but one of Austen's novels.

In a letter of 1847 Marian describes herself as a young lady who has been '*guanoing* her mind with French novels' (*L*, i, 234). The two principal cross-channel fertilisers were George Sand and Balzac. She read at least eight of the former's novels; concerning one of them, she begged Sara Hennell in 1849 to 'Send me the criticism of Jacques, the morn's morning, only beware there are not too many blasphemies against my divinity' (*L*, i, 275). Five days later, Marian elaborated on her extravagant admiration. It did not matter whether she agreed with Sand's 'moral code' or whether 'the design of her plot' was correct. What did matter was that it had been given to the French novelist 'to delineate human passion and its results . . . with such truthfulness such nicety of discrimination such tragic power and withal such loving gentle humour that one might live a century with nothing but one's own dull faculties' and not know as much about the subject as six of her pages suggested (*L*, i, 277–8).

There was an equal degree of familiarity with the novels of Balzac, described in 1855 as 'perhaps the most wonderful writer of fiction the world has ever seen' (*Essays*, 146). He was the other writer who had supplied too high a standard for novels of provincial life for one to be satisfied with inferior productions. His *Curé de Tours*, for example, was 'incomparable'. *César Birotteau* was read in 1856 and a sentence of narratorial generalisation copied into her notebook, as was a sentence from *Mémoires de deux jeunes mariées*. And a number of other Balzac novels were read in 1859, including *Père Goriot*, on which Marian made an extraordinary comment, to be considered below.

She was equally familiar with her English contemporaries. Letters from the 1840s, for example, show that she read Dickens' *Martin Chuzzlewit*, *Dombey and Son* and *David Copperfield* in the original monthly instalments. And *Little Dorritt*, then being serialised, is mentioned in the 1856 article on 'The Natural History of German Life'. There Dickens is described as the 'one great novelist' of contemporary Britain 'who is gifted with the utmost power of rendering the external traits of our town population', and who, if he could also render 'their psychological character – their conceptions of life, and their emotions – with the same truth as their idiom and manners', would make 'the greatest contribution Art has ever made to the awakening of social sympathies'. Unfortunately, Dickens 'scarcely ever passes from the humorous and external to the emotional and tragic, without being as transcendent in his unreality as he was a moment before in his truthfulness'. His 'frequently false psychology, his preternaturally virtuous poor children and artisans', all tended to foster 'the miserable fallacy that high morality and refined sentiment can grow out of harsh social relations, ignorance, and want' (*Essays*, 271–2).

In the next paragraph of the article, the Young England trilogy of Disraeli was criticised for its 'aristocratic dilettantism which attempts to restore the "good old times" by a sort of idyllic masquerading, and to grow feudal fidelity and veneration as we grow prize turnips, by an artificial system of culture' (*Essays*, 272). Marian had read *Coningsby*, *Sybil* and *Tancred* as they appeared during the 1840s. The second had led her to remark that the author 'hath good veins, as Bacon would say, but there is not enough blood in them'. The last seemed 'very "thin" and inferior in the working up' to the first two; and a correspondent was challenged to find 'any lofty meaning in it or any true picturing of life' (*L*, i, 193, 245, 241). Marian was more partial to the fiction of Elizabeth Gaskell, but no less critical. 'With all its merits', *Ruth* 'will not be an enduring or classical fiction'. The author was 'constantly misled by a love of sharp contrasts – of "dramatic" effects'. She was not content with 'the half tints of real life. Hence she agitates one for the moment, [but] does not secure one's lasting sympathy; her scenes and characters do not become typical'. Nonetheless, when Mrs Gaskell wrote in 1859 to congratulate the author of *Scenes of Clerical Life* and *Adam Bede*, Marian mentioned in her answer that 'while the question of my power was still undecided for me', she had been conscious 'that my feeling towards Life and Art had some affinity with the feeling which had inspired *Cranford* and the earlier chapters of *Mary Barton*' (*L*, ii, 86; iii, 198).

The references in the letters to Thackeray are more flattering. On the whole, Marian was inclined to regard him, 'as I suppose the majority of people with any intellect do, [as] the most powerful of living novelists' (*L*, ii, 349). The runner-up in her estimation seems to have been Charlotte Brontë, who was described in 1851 as 'perhaps the best' of all the modern English novelists. Marian had read *Jane Eyre* in 1848, the year after its publication. The book was interesting, she reported to Charles Bray, 'only I wish the characters would talk a little less like the heroes and heroines of police reports'. Moreover, while 'all self-sacrifice is good . . . one would like it to be in a somewhat nobler cause than that of a diabolical law which chains a man soul and body to a putrefying carcase'. *Villette*, read in 1853, was 'a still more wonderful book' than *Jane Eyre*; 'There is something almost preternatural in its power'. Lewes had told her that its author was 'a little, plain, provincial, sickly-looking old maid. Yet what passion, what fire in her! Quite as much as in George Sand, only the clothing is less voluptuous' (*L*, i, 355, 268; ii, 87, 91).

Most of the reviews of new novels that Marian wrote during the mid-1850s are found in the seven 'Belles Lettres' sections that she prepared for the *Westminster Review*. The task of the quarterly reviewer of new fiction could be likened to going mushrooming: 'picking up and throwing away heaps of dubious fungi' until an 'unmistakeable mushroom' was discovered: 'The plentiful dubious fungi are the ordinary quarter's crop of novels, not all poisonous, but generally not appetizing, and certainly not nourishing' (*WR*, 64 [1855], 288). There were several reasons why very few novels were unmistakable mushrooms. One was that 'the great mass of fictions are imitations more or less slavish and mechanical – imitations of Scott, of Balzac, of Dickens, of Currer Bell [Charlotte Brontë], and the rest of the real "makers"' (*WR*, 65 [1856], 638). Another was that the great majority of novels were topical and therefore ephemeral, never rising, 'above the dead level of the circulating library . . . They are the novels that flatter a prejudice, that speak the lingo of a clique, or that further the purposes of party propagandism'. These writers had 'none of that genius which is greater than its intentions [and] ends by giving a picture of life that endures when dogma and party are forgotten' (*WR*, 66 [1856], 258).

Technical proficiency, however, was not enough to make a novel into a mushroom. Charles Reade's *It's Never Too Late to Mend*, for example, had many of the necessary elements but nonetheless did not rise above the level of mere cleverness: 'we feel throughout the presence of remarkable talent, which makes effective use of materials, but nowhere of the genius which absorbs material, and reproduces it as a living whole, in which you do not admire the ingenuity of the workman, but the vital energy of the producer'. The latter 'lives *in* his characters'; the former 'remains outside them, and dresses them up.' Part of the problem was that Reade's habit of writing for the stage

    misleads him into seeking after those exaggerated contrasts and effects which are accepted as a sort of rapid symbolism by a theatrical audience, but are utterly out of place in a fiction, where the time and means for attaining a result are less limited, and an impression of character or purpose may be given more nearly as it is in real life – by a sum of less concentrated particulars.

(*Essays*, 329–30).

The causes of the failure of silly novels by lady novelists were more fundamental. The 'greatest deficiencies' of this considerable body of fiction were due 'hardly more to the want of intellectual power than to the want of those moral qualities that contribute to literary excellence – patient diligence, a sense of the responsibility involved in publication, and an appreciation of the sacredness of the writer's art'. For example, instead of showing 'the real drama of Evangelicalism [which] lies among the middle and lower classes' and instead of offering pictures of 'religious life among the industrial classes in England' (as Harriet Beecher Stowe had done for the American Negroes), Evangelical lady novelists preferred a more genteel *mise en scène* (*Essays*, 323, 319–20). Two novels by lady novelists were not at all silly but were nonetheless artistically deficient. Julia Kavanagh's *Rachel Gray* was a serious effort – 'not a story of a fine lady's sorrows wept into embroidered pocket-handkerchiefs', but a story set in 'that most prosaic stratum of society, the small shopkeeping class'. It concerned the trials of a dressmaker and a grocer. The author had undertaken to impress readers with 'the every-day sorrows of our commonplace fellow-men'. But for pathos and humour, this kind of novel depended on 'the delicate and masterly treatment of slight details, and in this sort of treatment it is utterly deficient'. Moreover, the piety of the title character was 'an abstract piety', quite unlike 'any true idea of piety as it exists in any possible dressmaker' (*Leader*, 5 January 1856, 19). Holme Lee's *Kathie Brand* epitomised yet another reason why the heap of discarded fungi was so large. The novel suffered from the same 'radical defect . . . which runs through ninety-nine novels out of every hundred'. It was most apparent in the author's handling of two striking incidents – a shipwreck and the burning of York Minster:

the author *writes about* [but] does not *paint* them. We feel that she was not present at either – she has not made them present to us. The reader sees nothing beyond the author's intention to produce an effect . . .

An analogous want of truth – or vivid realization – in the presentation of her characters and incidents, gives a blurred indistinctness to most parts of this novel . . . We do not live in the company of the personages; we do not hear them speak: we do not joy with them, and suffer with them . . . When the imagination is actively creating unusual characters and startling incidents, we do not so closely scrutinize probability and truthful representation; but when the imagination moves amidst ordinary realities, if it does not realize them vividly, the result is inevitable weariness.

(WR, 67 [1857], 321–2)

In her practical criticism, then, Marian identified a number of qualities that were prerequisites for the writing of novels that were unmistakable mushrooms. Her thinking about two of these qualities – realism and genius – now needs to be considered in more detail. There is nothing surprising about the emphasis on the former. A novel's truth to life, and the degree to which it was a picture of actual life, were the principal standards of judgement used by *Westminster Review* critics in the early 1850s, including George Henry Lewes. What is distinctive about Marian's employment of the criterion of realism is the way in which it is linked to questions of sympathy and fellow-feeling. The linkage is even closer in her first two fictional works, both of which contain extended passages of narratorial commentary promulgating the aesthetic of realism cum sympathy.

The first of them is found at the beginning of chapter 5 of *Amos Barton*, where the narrator heavily underlines the fact that her title character is 'in no respect an ideal or exceptional character [but] palpably and unmistakably commonplace'. Many of her readers will no doubt have become habituated to the ideal in fiction and will be reluctant to extend sympathy to 'a man who was so very far from remarkable'. Such readers 'would gain unspeakably if [they] would learn with me to see some of the poetry and the pathos, the tragedy and the comedy, lying in the experience of a human soul that looks out through dull grey eyes, and that speaks in a voice of quite ordinary tones'. Two chapters later, the narrator again emphasises her intention:

my only merit must lie in the faithfulness with which I represent to you the humble experience of an ordinary fellow-mortal. I wish to stir your sympathy with commonplace troubles – to win your tears for real sorrow: sorrow such as may live next door to you – such as walks neither in rags nor in velvet, but in very ordinary decent apparel.

In *Adam Bede*, a whole chapter is devoted to the realistic aesthetic: chapter 17, 'In Which the Story Pauses a Little'. Here the narrator answers an imagined interlocutor by insisting that her informing purpose is to give 'a faithful account of men and things as they have mirrored themselves in my mind'. It was for 'this rare, precious quality of truthfulness' that the narrator delighted 'in many Dutch paintings, which lofty-minded people despise'. Such representations were valuable because they helped one to learn to 'tolerate, pity, and love' the ordinary fellow-mortals among whom one lived. The narrator had herself come to the conclusion that 'human nature is lovable' and had 'learnt something of its deep pathos, its sublime mysteries' by having lived 'a great deal among people more or less commonplace and vulgar'. The stimulation of this fellow-feeling in art was dependent on realistic representation: 'therefore let us always have men ready to give the loving pains of a life to the faithful representing of commonplace things – men who . . . delight in showing how kindly the light of heaven falls on them'.

While these interpolations strike distinctive notes in English fiction, there are important non-fictional sources and analogues of the realism-cum-sympathy aesthetic, which is squarely in a major nineteenth-century tradition stemming from Wordsworth. In his Preface to the *Lyrical Ballads* Wordsworth explained that he had chosen 'low and rustic life' as his subject matter because 'the essential passions of the heart' and 'the great and simple affections of our nature' could be better seen in operation. The subject was important because 'at the present day' a multitude of causes were combining to dull one's sense of the passions, thoughts and feelings common to all human beings – 'the loss of friends and kindred', for example, or 'gratitude and hope . . . fear and sorrow'. And in book 13 of the 1850 *Prelude* Wordsworth had described the importance in his early experience of encountering ordinary humanity in the 'public way':

> When I began to enquire,
> To watch and question those I met, and speak

Without reserve to them, the lonely roads
Were open schools in which I daily read
With most delight the passions of mankind,
Whether by words, looks, sighs, or tears revealed;
There saw into the depth of human souls,
Souls that appear to have no depth at all
To careless eyes.

The same aesthetic credo is found in works by Browning and
Ruskin which were reviewed by Marian in her 'Belles Lettres'
articles, and which clearly influenced the development of her
realistic aesthetic. In her discussion of *Men and Women* she had
found room to quote some 150 lines of 'Fra Lippo Lippi', in which
the speaker, an early Renaissance painter, challenges the idealising
and moralising artistic conventions of his time, arguing that the
artist should be free to paint the actual visible world that he sees
before him – a world that through the painter's art others were
enabled to see as if for the first time:

Art was given for that –
God uses us to help each other so,
Lending our minds out.

In another article, Marian discussed the third volume of Ruskin's
Modern Painters. She endorsed its insistence that the fundamental
principles of art and of morality were the same and that 'in making
clear to ourselves what is best and noblest in art, we are making
clear to ourselves what is best and noblest in morals'. But the
aspect of Ruskin's work that Marian most emphasised was its
doctrine of realism:

The truth of infinite value that he teaches is *realism* – the doctrine
that all truth and beauty are to be attained by a humble and
faithful study of nature, and not by substituting vague forms,
bred by imagination on the mists of feeling, in place of definite,
substantial reality. The thorough acceptance of this doctrine
would remould our life.

(*WR*, 65 [1856], 626)

As has been recognised, there is a seeming problem with this
passage in that it does not accurately describe Ruskin's views on

realism and truth to nature. Ruskin, after all, not only attacked the false idealisations of the Grand Style; he was equally insistent that the imitative realism of the Dutch painters ('the various Van somethings and Back somethings') was inferior art. As early as 1840 he had insisted that 'each great artist conveys to you, not so much the scene, as the impression of the scene on his own originality of mind'. The same point is made in various ways in the third volume of *Modern Painters*: for example, in the distinction between 'the two schools of Lower and Higher art', the former of which 'merely copies what is set before it'; and in the insistence that 'great art is produced by men who think acutely and nobly'. There was a marked distinction between such art and that 'produced by men who do not feel at all, but who reproduce, though ever so accurately, yet coldly, like human mirrors, the scenes which pass before their eyes'.[1]

Marian's summary of Ruskin's truth of infinite value is, then, misleading. But the reason is rhetorical oversimplification, not naive views on representational art. It is clear from other texts that Marian makes the same crucial distinctions that Ruskin does and similarly emphasises the expressive and formative power of the artist. In 1854, during her stay at Weimar, she saw a number of busts and portraits of Goethe and noted that they were 'a proof, if any were wanted, [of] how inevitably subjective art is, even when it professes to be purely imitative – how the most active perception gives us rather a reflex of what we think and feel, than the real sum of objects before us' (*Essays*, 89). Moreover, we have already seen that in the seventeenth chapter of *Adam Bede* the narrator speaks of giving 'a faithful account of men and things as they have mirrored themselves in my mind' – that is, as they have been apprehended by her perception and sensibility. While the chapter may seem to offer Dutch painters as the image of the author of *Adam Bede*, the novel's opening sentence offers a very different image: 'the Egyptian sorcerer [who] undertakes to reveal to any chance comer far-reaching visions of the past'. In a letter of 1857 Marian observed that 'Art must be either real and concrete, or ideal and eclectic'. Both were 'good and true in their way', she said; but her fiction was 'of the former kind. I undertake to exhibit nothing as it should be; I only try to exhibit some things as they have been or are, seen through such a medium as my own nature gives me'. But it was the medium – the imagination and sensibility – that was of primary importance in the creative act. That is why Marian was so enraged by the suggestions that the scenes and characters in her early books were simply transcribed from life. 'How curious it seems to me', she wrote to Sara Hennell, 'that people should think Dinah's sermon, prayers, and speeches [in *Adam Bede*] were *copied* – when they were written with hot tears, as they surged up in my own mind!' As she explained to her publisher in 1861: there was a distinction to be made between 'the real and the imaginative': one 'could not have the former without the latter and greater quality. Any real observation of life and character must be limited, and the imagination must fill in and give life to the picture' (*L*, ii, 362; iii, 176, 427).

Unfortunately, in her essays of the 1850s Marian has little to say about the nature and genesis of imaginative power. She would later employ a scientific vocabulary in speaking about the creative process; but at this time she relied on long familiar tropes: 'genius', 'creative power', 'creative impulse', 'innate power', a vague reference to 'that vigour of conception and felicity of expression, by which we distinguish the undefinable something called genius' (*Essays*, 47). One way to have explored this power would have been to analyse her own creative processes, as Wordsworth had done in the *Prelude*, in which he employs the same vocabulary as does Marian. But she was on the brink of becoming, not a subjective poet whose subject matter was his/her own creative processes, but a writer of realistic, representational prose fiction. Marian takes genius as a given and seems unconcerned with questions of where it comes from and why some people have it and others do not. She does, however, make a remarkable comment in an 1848 letter on its mode of operation in the nineteenth century. 'Artistic power', she reflects, seems 'to resemble dramatic power – to be an intuitive perception of the varied states of which the human mind is susceptible with ability to give them out anew in intensified expression'. It was true that 'the older the world gets, originality becomes less possible. Great subjects are used up, and civilization tends evermore to repress individual predominance, highly-wrought agony or ecstatic joy'. This was not a cause for creative dismay, however; for 'the gentler emotions will be ever new . . . and genius will probably take their direction' (*L*, i, 247–8).

The dominant imaginative coloration in the mirror of the early George Eliot novels is precisely a passionate concern with these ever-new gentler emotions, the 'sweet charities which are found in the details of ordinary life' (*Essays*, 371). Her most direct and compelling statement of the unique value of this kind of art occurs in 'The Natural History of German Life':

> The greatest benefit we owe to the artist, whether painter, poet, or novelist, is the extension of our sympathies. Appeals founded on generalizations and statistics require a sympathy ready-made, a moral sentiment already in activity; but a picture of human life such as a great artist can give, surprises even the trivial and the selfish into that attention to what is apart from themselves, which may be called the raw material of moral sentiment . . . Art is the nearest thing to life; it is a mode of amplifying experience and extending our contact with our fellow-men beyond the bounds of our personal lot.
>
> (*Essays*, 270–1)

The value of art was not that it was didactic and contained moral lessons. In fact, minds which were 'pre-eminently didactic – which insist on a "lesson" and despise everything that will not convey a moral [were] deficient in sympathetic emotion' and could therefore not create the pictures of human life that were the greatest benefit owed to the artist (*Essays*, 379). This was the trouble with the fiction of Charles Kingsley. His 'fierce antagonism and his perpetual hortative tendency' were the 'grand mistakes' that enfeebled all his novels: 'If he would confine himself to his true sphere, he might be a teacher in the sense in which every great artist is a teacher – namely, by giving us his higher sensibility as a medium, a delicate acoustic or optical instrument, bringing home to our coarser senses what would otherwise be unperceived by us' (*Essays*, 126). The greatness of Rousseau's writing was found precisely in his higher sensibility. The French writer's views on 'life, religion, and government [were] miserably erroneous', but his genius nonetheless sent an electric thrill through Marian's 'intellectual and moral frame which has awakened me to new perceptions, which has made man and nature a fresh world of thought and feeling to me – and this not by teaching me any new belief'.

It was furthermore the case that the impact of Rousseau's genius was unaffected by the fact that he was guilty of some of the worst basenesses 'that have degraded civilized man' (*L*, i, 277). The same was true of novels that depicted morally questionable material – at least when the novel was Goethe's *Wilhelm Meister*, the morality of which Marian defended in an 1855 article in the *Leader*. But there were limits to her realistic aesthetic, and Balzac, wonderful writer of fiction though he was, 'has in many of his novels overstepped this limit. He drags us by his magic force through scene after scene of unmitigated vice, till the effect of walking among this human carrion is a moral nausea' (*Essays*, 146).

In 1859 Marian recorded in her journal: 'We have just finished reading aloud "Père Goriot," a hateful book' (Cross, ii, 104). Some light is thrown on this cryptic statement by a passage in a letter Marian had written the previous year:

> The soul of art lies in its treatment and not in its subject . . . The Heart of Midlothian would probably have been thought highly objectionable if a skeleton of the story had been given by a writer whose reputation did not place him above question. And the same story told by a Balzacian French writer would probably have made a book that no young person could read without injury.
>
> (*L*, viii, 201)

As it happens, in *Père Goriot*, Balzac's narrator had himself cited the same novel of Walter Scott in a reflexive passage concerning the career of Rastignac, the young man who is one of the novel's central subjects. *The Heart of Midlothian* was a 'masterpiece' containing in Jeanie Deans and her father two 'magnificent figures of integrity'. But in 'the lax moral state which is characteristic of this epoch', one met 'more rarely than in any previous age' with such exemplary figures. The narrator was therefore led to raise the possibility that 'a work of the converse kind' that depicted the moral corruption of its central character could be 'not less fine, nor less dramatic'.[2] For Marian the answer was clearly that such a work could not be as fine unless the treatment of the subject allowed for the extension of the reader's sympathies. As she had asserted in her article on *Wilhelm Meister*, 'the novelist may place before us every aspect of human life where there is some trait of love, or endurance, or helplessness to call forth our best sympathies' (*Essays*, 146). It was, therefore, not the qualities present in *Père Goriot*, but the qualities absent from the novel, that made it a 'hateful book'. The letter in which Marian had located the soul of art was signed 'George Eliot' and was written three months after the publication of *Scenes of Clerical Life*, in which her realistic aesthetic was first put to the test.

In November 1856 Lewes had approached John Blackwood, the Edinburgh publisher, concerning a manuscript written, so he claimed, by a clerical friend. It was the first of a proposed series of 'tales and sketches illustrative of the actual life of our country clergy about a quarter of a century ago: but solely in its *human* and *not at all* in its *theological* aspect' (*L*, ii, 269). Blackwood had liked the story, as well as two further sketches from the same unknown pen. They were published in instalments in *Blackwood's Magazine* during 1857 and in book form in January 1858 as *Scenes of Clerical Life* by George Eliot. In their correspondence regarding the stories, Blackwood must have been impressed with his new author's clarity of intention and self-assurance. We have already noted Marian's rejection of his suggestion that the colours used in the depiction of Milby in the third of the stories were 'a little harsh'; and when he suggested some changes in characterisation in the second story, the reply was unequivocal: 'I am unable to alter anything in relation to the delineation or development of character, as my stories always grow out of my psychological conception of the dramatis personae'. She could not 'stir a step aside from what I *feel* to be *true* in character'. As an artist, she would be 'utterly power-less if I departed from my own conceptions of life and character' (*L*, ii, 299, 348).

The three stories themselves convey the same sense of assur-ance. Both the places and the persons that make up the *Scenes of Clerical Life* are copiously and vividly rendered. There is Shepperton Church 'as it was in the old days, with its outer coat of rough stucco, its red-tiled roof' and 'heterogeneous windows patched with desultory bits of painted glass'; Cross Farm, where Mrs Patten, a childless old lady, lives with her niece, for whom she cherishes a 'blood relation's hatred' and whose expectation of a large legacy 'she is determined to disappoint' (*Amos Barton*, ch. 1); the little rural church at Knebly where farmers' families come through miry lanes to attend Sunday afternoon services; the work-house, a large square stone building on the only elevation of ground for miles around; the bar of the Red Lion in the market town of Milby, where the town's lawyers, its two medical prac-titioners, and other men of a certain standing gather to drink and talk; the Milby vicarage, where the district clergymen who hold monthly meetings include 'a very dyspeptic and evangelical man, who . . . thinks the immense sale of the "Pickwick Papers", re-cently completed, one of the strongest proofs of original sin' (*Amos*

Barton, ch. 6); the lovingly described garden of Mr Jerome, a retired corn factor and leading member of the Independent chapel; and the dismal area of Paddiford Common on the outskirts of the town where Mrs Linnet and her two daughters, then only in the 'temperate zone of old-maidism', are joined for tea by Miss Pratt, the one blue-stocking in Milby, who had reached the 'arctic region' of that condition (*Janet's Repentance*, ch. 3).

This richly textured world is common to the three *Scenes*. What is distinctive about each is the mode of presentation – the formal and generic means used to convey the sense of what the author feels to be true in character and to call forth in the reader a sympathetic emotional response. These different schemata may be regarded as a series of experiments in combining realistic representation with the extension of the reader's sympathies and in charging commonplace things with an affective intensity. As such, while none of them is a complete success, each is interesting, and each has its distinctive features.

As analogues and precedents for the *Scenes of Clerical Life*, Lewes in his letter to Blackwood had cited Goldsmith's *Vicar of Wakefield* and Jane Austen; while the reviewer in *The Times* attempted to fix the location of the *Scenes* by triangulation: the 'early days' of Galt or Lockhart; Crabbe in a 'softer mood'; and the paintings of David Wilkie (*CH*, 62). In the case of the first story, *Amos Barton*, however, the antecedent works it most closely resembles, and the ones to which it may be most instructively compared, are the lyrical ballads and related poems of Wordsworth. Like the story of Margaret in the first book of the *Excursion*, that of Amos Barton is

a common tale,
An ordinary sorrow of man's life,
A tale of silent suffering.

Just as Wordsworth's poems often centre on the loss of a loved one – a husband, son, daughter or brother – so Marian's common tale turns on the death of Milly Barton, which leaves her husband desolate and their brood of young children motherless. *Amos Barton* employs the same devices that Wordsworth uses in bringing his pathetic subject matter into sharp focus and increasing the affective intensity. One of them is to help show the reader how to react by describing the story's effect on a person or persons within the poem (usually the narrator). Marian adapts this device in showing how the villagers of Shepperton are moved to sympathy by the plight of Amos, who had failed to touch 'the spring of goodness' in his parishioners through his sermons, but 'touched it effectually by his sorrows' (ch. 10). A second Wordsworthian strategy is direct address by the narrator to the reader – either apostrophes or reflexive comments calculated to break down the reader's habitual responses and conventional expectations and open him to the power of the pathetic story. 'Look at him as he winds through the little churchyard', exclaims the narrator in chapter 2, shifting to the present tense for added emphasis, just as Wordsworth does in 'The Old Cumberland Beggar'; and we have already remarked in on the interpolated comments in which the narrator speaks of her desire 'to win your tears for real sorrow'.

The third and most important Wordsworthian device adapted in *Amos Barton* is the supersession of narrative by an intensely emotional moment or incident. This fundamental Wordsworthian strategy is called attention to in the very title *Lyrical Ballads*, which points up the distinctive combination of narrative (ballad) and an intense emotional (lyrical) passage. Just as 'Simon Lee', after ten stanzas of background concerning the aged title character, concludes with three stanzas describing an affecting 'incident', so *Amos Barton* concludes with three short chapters describing Milly Barton's death and burial, chapters in which the creative power of Marian Evans is impressively instanced for the first time.

In the story's early chapters, the narratorial voice had been intermittently ponderous and awkward. At times there had been rather too much erudite wit, and too many learned allusions and polysyllabic words for a story of commonplace troubles. 'Supererogatory', 'differentiated' (in the scientific sense), and 'unfecundatedness' were almost as distracting as two quoted lines of Sophocles' Greek. And the comparisons of Amos' teeth to the remnants of Napoleon's old guard and his oratory to a Belgian railroad horn were too clever by half. In addition, other places were weakened by sentimental touches in the presentation of Milly, the incarnation of the 'soothing, unspeakable charm of gentle womanhood' with its 'sublime capacity of loving' (ch. 2).

In the last three chapters, these apprentice crudities vanish, as telling is replaced by showing and generalisations by acute psychological notation. Blackwood had thought the death of Milly powerfully done but wondered whether it wasn't spoiled a little by specifying so minutely the different Barton children and their thoughts as their mother's coffin is lowered into the grave. He was wrong once again and the author right in replying that this particularisation has 'an important effect on the imagination' (*L*, ii, 288). Marian was just as sure-footed in the previous chapter in restricting the reader to an outside view of Amos as he arrives in the room where his wife lies dying. And the final broken sentences he is given to speak when he throws himself on his wife's grave and kisses the cold turf on the night before he and his children are to leave Shepperton forever could not be bettered: 'Milly, Milly, dost thou hear me? I didn't love thee enough – I wasn't tender enough to thee – but I think of it all now' (ch. 10).

Mr. Gilfil's Love Story, the second of the *Scenes*, moves towards the same climactic moment of intense pathos – the death of a beloved wife that leaves the clergyman husband devastated. But the means to the end are very different, as are the corresponding levels of intensity. The opening chapter of the story and its brief epilogue are set in the 1820s, the time of the title character's old age, when he has long been a revered figure in Shepperton. It is intimated, however, that 'like many a bent old man, or a wizened old woman, Maynard Gilfil had in the distant past experienced an intensity of emotion of which the diminished present is little better than 'wood-ashes'.

The intervening chapters, set forty years earlier, reveal that in his young manhood Mr Gilfil had experienced a love all the more deep and intense because it was a first love of the strongest and most enduring kind: 'that which begins in childish companionship' (ch. 4). After vicissitudes and sorrows, this love is at last requited; but Maynard Gilfil and Caterina tasted only 'a few months of perfect happiness' before the bride, a delicate plant, died 'in the struggle to put forth a blossom' (ch. 21). The stronger and more deeply rooted bridegroom survived, but (in the closing image of the story) 'it is with men as with trees'; if the finest branches are lopped off while the young sap is flowing, what might have been a grand tree will become 'but a whimsical misshapen trunk'.

So far, so good; the problem with *Mr. Gilfil's Love Story* is in the disproportion between the *then* and the *now* parts of the story. Maynard Gilfil is the centre of attention only in the twelve-page opening chapter and the one-page epilogue. In the close to hundred intervening pages, he is only intermittently present and then mainly in the ancillary roles of confidant or factotum. Moreover, the extended flashback is different in setting, subject and treatment both from the framing chapters and from anything else in the *Scenes*. The setting is Cheverel Manor, the home of Sir Christopher Cheverel, 'as fine a specimen of the English gentleman as could be found in those venerable days' (ch. 2). Both he and the other gentry characters all seem drawn less from life, let alone ordinary life, than from literature – more particularly from the pages of Jane Austen, whom Marian was rereading during the composition of the story. Misunderstandings and complications arise because Captain Wybrow, the heir to the estate, has trifled with the affections of Caterina, the Italian-born ward of Sir Christopher, who is the central character in the country house narrative and tilts it heavily in the direction of melodrama. Caterina's exotic background, fragility, uncontrollable passion and savage jealousy are all played up. There is a dagger; there is the decision to kill Wybrow; there is the Captain lying dead from natural causes at their place of rendezvous; there is her disappearance, her remorse, her eventual unburdening of herself to Gilfil and their short-lived union.

In the story the mixture of Jane Austen marriage plot and sentimental melodrama is the opposite of synergistic. The narrative is competently managed and there is evidence of other novelistic skills. But there is little intensity, a deficiency that seems owing to the fact that Marian had strayed rather too far from the quotidian aesthetic of *Amos Barton*. Indeed, the country house parts of *Mr. Gilfil* recall the ironic reference of the narrator of the former story to learning from the newspapers that, in contrast to the 'homely details' of her story, 'many remarkable novels, full of striking situations, thrilling incidents, and eloquent writing, have appeared . . . within the last season' (ch. 5).

It is not surprising that something very different was attempted in the third and last of *Scenes of Clerical Life*. In *Janet's Repentance* the trigger of pathos is once again the death of a loved one; in fact there are two bereavements in the story. Janet Dempster first loses her once-loved husband and then at the story's end says goodbye to the dying Evangelical clergyman Edgar Tryan, who had brought her succour in her hour of deepest need and whom she had come to love. But while the pathetic pivot is similar, the content and the method of *Janet's Repentance* are different from its predecessors. For one thing, there is a more fully articulated social world, and the society depicted is changing rather than static. The action is set at a particular historical moment, of which its central events are an epitome: the impact of Evangelicalism on a provincial town in the Midlands in the 1830s. And for the first time in Marian's fiction, the interaction of private life and public life is studied.

Another difference is the richer thematic texture; for example, the question of natural versus supernatural causation. Janet's mother believes in the transcendent 'eternal love' of the unseen Christian God. But in referring to this belief, the narrator comments that while we reap what we sow, 'Nature has love over and above that justice, and gives us shadow and blossom and fruit that spring from no planting of ours' (ch. 5). This would seem to suggest the existence of some transpersonal but not transcendent force, exemplified in the operation of what the narrator later calls 'the deep-down fibrous roots of human love and goodness' (ch. 7).

The central testing ground for these alternative possibilities is the story of Janet and her repentance. In chapter 15 she prays for a ray of hope to pierce the 'horrible gloom' of her life so that she may come to believe 'in a Divine love – in a heavenly Father who cared for His children'. Through Tryan she does recover her belief in what she calls the unseen elements in the divine will. But is the cause of her spiritual regeneration the unseen *divine* workings to which Tryan has made her receptive, or is it rather the case that his human kindness and concern have caused the stirrings of some regenerating *human* feeling in her? The narrator reports that there was a 'divine love' and an 'Infinite Love' caring for Janet (chs. 21, 25); but the narratorial mode of these notations is *style indirect libre*: what Janet thought about her condition is reported, but not necessarily what the narrator thought. On the other hand, the narrator does seem to be speaking *in propria persona* in two passages where it is suggested that the relation of natural to supernatural love is that of lower to higher: that human sympathy prepares the soul for that stronger leap by which faith grasps the idea of divine sympathy.

The ambivalence displayed in the text on this key question is the most striking thematic feature of *Janet's Repentance*. It is surely not what one would have expected from the author given that at the time of writing Marian was a firm believer in Feuerbachian doctrines which regarded supernatural causation as the illusion and human agency as the reality. The explanation of this ambivalence, I believe, has to do with difficulties in the calculations of the realism-cum-sympathy aesthetic, and with predispositions in Marian's sensibility that lead to the title character's being idealised.

Janet Dempster is in fact an early sketch of Romola, the stylised and idealised title character of the fourth George Eliot novel. (The majestic, enduring, and tableau-like quality of her beauty anticipates that of the later Florentine heroine, as does her position as the childless wife of a bad husband whose dominance gives way to that of a charismatic preacher who leads the heroine to a life of charity and good works.) In both characters there is a certain strain of visionary possibility that is discontinuous with realistic presentation. Thus, at the end of her story, Janet and the equally idealised Tryan are allowed to share 'a sacred kiss of promise' that he will not look for her in vain at the last (ch. 27). This allows her to live the remainder of her life sustained by *both* divine and human guidance: 'She walked in the presence of unseen witnesses – of the Divine Love that had rescued her, of the human love that waited for its eternal repose until it had seen her endure to the end' (ch. 28). This ending is affecting and one would not have it otherwise. But if it is miles away from silly clerical novels by lady novelists, it is almost as far removed from the dull-grey-eyes and voice-of-quite-ordinary-tones realism of *Amos Barton*. And it is just as far from Marian's mature moral credo that the highest calling is to do without opium.

In January 1857 Marian's last 'Belles Lettres' article appeared in the *Westminster Review*; the following September she informed Blackwood that *Janet's Repentance* would be the last of the clerical-life scenes. She had in mind a subject that 'will not come under the limitations of the title "Clerical Life"' and that she was 'inclined to take a large canvas for it, and write a novel' (*L*, ii, 381).

4

Adam Bede (1858) and *Silas Marner* (1861)

What strikes me in *Adam Bede* is the attentive, meticulous, respectful, poetic and sympathetic portrayal of the humblest, most hard-working life . . . And also the sense of the gravity of an evil intention, of a failure of the will whose dire repercussions are borne everywhere by the solidarity among human creatures, and the sense of the mysterious grandeur of human life and the life of nature, of the sublime mysteries of which we are part though as little conscious of it as the flower that grows (cf., *Silas Marner*) . . . Extremely keen feeling for nature which animates rather than depicts it. Especially in its tranquillity . . . Exact, picturesque, witty, eloquent way of making caricatural characters speak without caricature . . . Feeling for how things and our hearts change over a lifetime. Return of Silas to [Lantern] Yard, etc. In places, proof of a good knowledge of philosophy.

Marcel Proust

In August 1859 Marian Evans noted that 'at present my mind works with the most freedom and the keenest sense of poetry in my remotest past'. Two examples of this predisposition of her creative mind during her first years as a novelist are the genesis of her first and third novels. The 'germ' of *Adam Bede*, begun in October 1857, was an anecdote told her by her Methodist aunt one afternoon at Griff in 1839; while *Silas Marner*, on which work was begun in August 1860, 'unfolded itself from the merest millet-seed of thought': the 'recollection of having once, in early childhood, seen a linen-weaver with a bag on his back' and an 'expression of face' that led her to think 'he was an alien from his fellows' (*L*, iii, 128–9; ii, 502; iii, 371, 382, 427).

But unlike the *Scenes of Clerical Life*, which also sprang from early memories, *Adam Bede* and *Silas Marner* are set further back in time than the remote personal past of Marian Evans. Both offer richly detailed pictures of traditional rural life in the Midlands at the close of the eighteenth century, some two decades before their author was born. *Adam Bede*, 'a country story – full of the breath of cows and the scent of hay', is set in Hayslope, a village in a rich, undulating district of Loamshire; while *Silas Marner*, 'a story of old-fashioned village life' is set in Raveloe, a community nestled in a well-wooded hollow in an equally fertile part of the rich central plain of England (*L*, ii, 387; iii, 371).

One reason for Marian's interest in these pre-nineteenth-century village cultures was her concern, shared with Lewes, Spencer and other mid-century thinkers, with the decline of a sense of community in Victorian Britain. A key distinction in their thinking was that between two different types of social organisation – 'community' and 'society'. The former term referred to organic agricultural units with stable hierarchical stratifications of rank that were 'modelled on the family and rooted in the traditional and the sacred'; the latter denoted heterogeneous urban aggregates, divided along shifting class lines and 'shaped by the rational pursuit of self-interest in a capitalistic and secular environment'.[1] Marian's concern with this subject had been stimulated by the *Naturgeschichte* of Wilhelm Heinrich von Riehl, two of whose studies of the German peasantry had been the subject of her long 1856 review essay, 'The Natural History of German Life'. The close connections between this essay and both *Adam Bede* and *Silas Marner* are clear from the following passage, in which Marian remarks that in order for her English readers to appreciate what Riehl is saying about the German peasantry,

we must remember what tenant-farmers and small proprietors were in England half a century ago, when the master helped to milk his own cows, and the daughters got up at one o'clock in the morning to brew, – when the family dined in the kitchen with the servants, and sat with them round the kitchen fire in the evening. In those days, the quarried parlour was innocent of a carpet, and its only specimens of art were a framed sampler and the best teaboard; the daughters even of substantial farmers had often no greater accomplishment in writing and spelling than they could procure at a dame-school; and, instead of carrying on sentimental correspondence, they were spinning their future table-linen, and looking after every saving in butter and eggs that might enable them to add to the little stock of plate and china which they were laying in against their marriage.

(*Essays*, 273)

The daughters in the second half of this passage prefigure Nancy and Priscilla Lammeter, the children of a gentleman farmer in *Silas Marner*; while the first half anticipates the picture in *Adam Bede* of the life of the Poyser family at the Hall Farm, though its farm yard, kitchen garden and dairy are described as well as its kitchen, and farm labourers as well as servants are shown eating with the family – meals that include cold veal, fresh lettuce and stuffed chine on one occasion, a plate of cold broad beans on another, and roast beef and fresh-drawn ale during the harvest supper.

It is just as telling that the defining characteristics of the traditional rural societies described by Riehl – rank, custom, the conservative spirit, and co-operation or community – are all abundantly illustrated in the two novels. Rank was one's inherited position in the organic structure of society, the psychological and historical roots of which went very deep. Squire Cass, for example, the principal personage among the petty gentry of Raveloe, 'had been used to parish homage all his life, used to the presupposition that his family, his tankards, and everything that was his, were the oldest and best; and as he never associated with any gentry higher than himself, his opinion was not disturbed by comparison' (ch. 9). And in *Adam Bede* it is the title character's attitude to rank – his deference to his betters and the 'large fund of reverence in his nature, which inclined him to admit all established claims' – that causes the narrator to remind the reader that Adam 'had the blood of the peasant in his veins, and that since he was in his prime half a century ago, you must expect some of his characteristics to be obsolete' (ch. 16).

For the peasant, custom (tradition and hereditary attachments) was more important than abstractions or individual feelings. In the two novels there are detailed descriptions of a number of customary occasions and activities which foster the sense of community, reaffirm the existing social order and give a sustaining sense of continuity in time. Secular examples in *Adam Bede* include the young squire's coming-of-age feast, to which five chapters are devoted, and the harvest supper described near the end of the novel, which is the climax of the annual cycle of communal agricultural activities that gives a pronounced seasonal rhythm to rural life. And in *Silas Marner* there is a long and colourful account of the annual new year's dance at Squire Cass's: its climax comes when the dancing begins in the accustomed way: 'That was as it should be – that was what everybody had been used to – and the charter of Raveloe seemed to be renewed by the ceremony' (ch. 11). It is the customary element in religion that makes it such a powerful force in the community and in an individual's life. In *Silas Marner* it is through his appropriation of 'the forms and customs of belief which were the mould of Raveloe life' that the title's character's regeneration becomes complete. Silas is shown to benefit greatly through coming to share in 'the observances held sacred by his neighbours' (chs. 16, 14). And in chapter 18 of *Adam Bede*, participation in the Sunday service is shown to be for Adam, who is mourning his father's death, 'the best channel he could have found for his mingled regret, yearning, and resignation; its interchange of beseeching cries for help, with outbursts of faith and praise – its recurrent responses and the familiar rhythm of its collects, seemed to speak for him as no other form of worship could have done'.

As the above examples suggest, both novels contain predominantly positive representations of traditional rural life in the Midlands. Given that the aesthetic flags under which both novels sail is faithful-representing-of-commonplace-things-realism, and that the narrators of both make strong, if implicit, claims to be serious social historians, it would not be unreasonable to ask how accurate and inclusive the representations are. After all, Marian Evans could have had no first-hand experience of the turn-of-the-century communities she depicts. It has been pointed out that in neither novel is there any indication of 'the vast upheavals in rural life which typify the 1790s'[2]; and while Henry James found that the novels contained 'strong internal evidence of truthfulness', he also thought their 'atmosphere too redolent of peace and abundance', and wondered about the fact that there were no instances 'of gross misery of any kind not directly caused by the folly of the sufferer. There are no pictures of vice or poverty or squalor. There are no rags, no gin, no brutal passions'.[3] Indeed, such features seem deliberately excluded from the worlds of *Silas Marner* and *Adam Bede*. Molly Farren, the alcoholic, opium-addicted wife of Godfrey Cass, who cherishes 'no higher memories than those of a barmaid's paradise of pink ribbons and gentlemen's jokes' (ch. 12), dies in the snow in her dirty rags on the outskirts of Raveloe. And after her crime and disgrace, Hetty Sorrell disappears not only from the pages of *Adam Bede* but also from the thoughts of the characters (except for Adam).

On the other hand, it is worth remembering that when he first visited Warwickshire, Thomas Carlyle was struck by the natural fertility of the land, which seemed, in comparison with the harsh soil of his native Scotland, to have 'a touch of paradise'.[4] One might further note that there are similar contrasts *within* the two novels. North of Raveloe lies a great manufacturing town in a dismal corner of which, near a jail and past bad-smelling alleys and doorways from which sallow, begrimed faces look out, is found the place where the narrow religious sect to which Silas Marner had belonged once assembled. And not far from the lush fields of Loamshire lies Stonyshire, in which is located the grim and unsheltered town of Snowfield, with its cotton mill in which Dinah Morris is employed.

After a point, however, it would be just as tendentious to pursue such a line of argument as it would be to insist on the historical omissions in these two fictional texts. *Adam Bede* and *Silas Marner* are novels, and their socio-historical representations should not be considered apart from their other informing concerns. The epigraphs to both novels do not come from Riehl; they are taken from poems of Wordsworth and their subject is the potentially positive effect on the human sympathies of a fallen woman in one case and a small child in the other. The principal aesthetic concern in both novels is the extension of the reader's sympathies through the faithful representing of ordinary life – the very subject Marian had discussed at the opening of 'The Natural History of German Life'. Later in the essay she had remarked that 'a return to the habits of peasant life [would be] the best remedy for many moral as well as physical diseases induced by perverted civilization' (*Essays*, 280–1). If one could not do this literally (for example, by emigrating to the other side of the ocean), the next best thing would be to be imaginatively transported back to an earlier socio-cultural world by an author intent – as Marian described her purpose in writing *Silas Marner* – on setting 'in a strong light the remedial influences of pure, natural human relations' (*L*, iii, 382).

Like the five other George Eliot novels, *Adam Bede* and *Silas Marner* employ an intrusive omniscient narrator. This presence is the single most important technical feature that the seven novels have in common. It is what more than anything else holds together and modulates the various other elements of which each novel is composed. One of the most noticeable features of this narratorial mode is its intrusive commentary. Sometimes these interruptions are both felicitous and telling; for example, the end of chapter 14 of *Silas Marner*:

> In old days there were angels who came and took men by the hand and led them away from the city of destruction. We see no white-winged angels now. But yet men are led away from threatening destruction: a hand is put into theirs, which leads them forth gently towards a calm and bright land, so that they no more look backward; and the hand may be a little child's.

The tenor of this passage is Feuerbachian: the supersession of a putatively divine causation by human instrumentality. But its largely monosyllabic simplicity also recalls the blank verse of Wordsworth's 'Michael', which supplies the novel's epigraph. And like its simplicity, the proverbial ring of the passage is perfectly adapted to a story with legendary overtones about common people and pure, natural human relations.

At other times, however, intrusive commentary can be distinctly infelicitous. A small-scale example occurs in chapter 29 of *Adam Bede* when the narrator cannot resist an utterly redundant parenthetical sarcasm concerning a character's attempt to placate his conscience: 'Pity that consequences are determined not by excuses but by actions!' A more conspicuous example is the page-long encomium to 'Old Leisure' in chapter 52. This 'wretched piece', as Raymond Williams complained, offers 'a sleepy fantasy of the past' in the personified figure of a contemplative, rather stout old gentleman of excellent digestion, 'a class figure who can afford to saunter' and whose leisure is dependent upon 'the sweat of other men's work'.[5] This whimsical intrusion is not simply gratuitous; it is also undermining of the more realistic presentation of rural life in the body of the novel.

Intrusive narratorial commentary had been found in such distinguished antecedent novelists as Fielding, Scott and Thackeray. But since the time when Jamesian and Flaubertian canons of impersonal narration became influential, these intrusions have had a counterproductive effect on many readers of the George Eliot novels. For James, the principal objection to such interventions was that they destroyed the narrative illusion by reminding readers that what they had before them was a fictitious construct. James, however, did not distinguish between two different kinds of intrusive narrators – distancing narrators and engaging narrators – and as a result was ill-equipped to appreciate how some novelists used the latter in order to add to the sense of reality of their narratives. In *Adam Bede*, for example, intrusive commentary, including direct addresses to the reader, is used to establish a sympathetic bond between the reader and the characters, and to emphasise the similarities between the novel's world and the reader's.

Even the most extended narratorial intrusion in the novel, chapter 17, 'In Which the Story Pauses a Little', can be seen to serve this end. When the narrator mentions that the source of certain information she possesses is Adam Bede, to whom she spoke in his old age, the boundary between the novel's fictional world and the real world of the reader grows appreciably fainter. Implicitly, the reader is being asked to receive the opinions of the narrator in the same way that she has taken in Adam's observations about one of the clerical successors of Mr Irwine. So, too, when the narrator directly addresses the reader, not with a reminder, in the manner of Thackeray or Trollope, that the characters are subject to authorial whim, but to persuade him/her 'to be in perfect charity' towards Mr Irwine, 'far as he may be from satisfying your demands on the clerical character'. And elsewhere in the chapter, the reader is invited, so to speak, to cross the boundary between the two worlds and join forces with the narrator in the necessary human enterprise of tolerating, pitying, and loving one's fellow man.[6]

There is a particular kind of narratorial commentary that is a distinctive feature of the George Eliot novels and an essential constituent of them: the discursive moral and psychological generalisations – the sayings, sententiae, maxims and dicta – that are an essential tool of characterisation, are closely linked to the dramatic and narrative situation, and are another important stimulus (though a more reflective one) to the interaction of text and reader. One cluster of examples are the comments in *Adam Bede* concerning early love. They will be presently examined, but it is better first to consider the moral and psychological dicta in relation to the most crucial single feature in the George Eliot novels of the omniscient narratorial mode: the employment of psychological omniscience. This device allows for the provision of various kinds of inside information: a particular movement of consciousness or moment of choice can be detailed; a summary can be provided of a character's private history; character profiles can be provided, ranging from sketches to detailed portraits; hidden motives can be revealed; and judgements can be rendered. The quality and kind of attention that a character receives from the psychologically omniscient narrator is a crucial aspect of his/her characterisation and of the reader's sense of the character; and there can be important thematic implications as well. This is just as true of the rustic characters in *Adam Bede* and *Silas Marner* as it is of the more complex central characters of the later novels. In fact, the comparative simplicity of the characters and (in some cases) the comparative crudity of their characterisation make it easier to identify and exemplify most of the varieties of psychological omniscience employed by the narrators.

Let us take *Adam Bede* as an example. One of its four principal characters is the well-intentioned but irresolute Arthur Donnithorne. On his first appearance in chapter 5, the reader is given a generic, outside view ('If you want to know more particularly how he looked, call to your remembrance some tawny-whiskered, brown-locked, clear-complexioned young Englishman whom you have met with in a foreign town'). It is not until chapter 12 that the point of view moves inside; but here the narrator is largely content to report what Arthur thinks of himself (for example, 'he had an agreeable confidence that his faults were all of a generous kind') rather than to offer a more penetrating assessment, and to maintain the generic frame of reference. By the end of chapter 16, when Arthur has begun to feel the opposing pulls of right conduct and desire for Hetty, a deeper inside view is offered in which the narrator speculates on Arthur's motivation in a way that the subject himself could not. And in chapter 26, a deeper stratum of the young man's being is momentarily illuminated not through analysis or speculation but through acute psychological notation. During the dancing at his coming-of-age feast Arthur at one point looks at Hetty and is struck by her expression, which makes him realise that she loves him all too well. This recognition oppresses him 'with a dread which yet had something of a terrible unconfessed delight in it . . . at that moment he felt he would have given up three years of his youth for the happiness of abandoning himself without remorse to his passion for Hetty'. The narrator attempts to explain this powerful reaction by means of a peculiar generalisation about certain faces that nature charges with a meaning and a pathos that do not belong to the individual but rather smack of the 'joys and sorrows of foregone generations'. But this is surely a mystification; what Arthur is experiencing, as psychological notation makes clear, is the destabilising intensity of raw sexual desire. (This is one of the comparatively few places in the George Eliot canon where the omniscient narrator's *telling* seems out of phase with her *showing*.) Finally, in chapter 29, by which time Arthur can no longer disguise from himself the seriousness of his having trifled with Hetty's affections, narratorial omniscience is employed to give a close and authoritative moral scrutiny; and moral dicta are provided concerning 'the terrible coercion in our deeds'.

Compared with Arthur's, the characterisation of Hetty Sorrell is so heavy-handed that it has long raised questions concerning the narrator's impartiality and even her good faith. The characterisation of the title character of *Adam Bede* differs from that of Arthur and Hetty in that Adam enjoys a privileged position *vis-à-vis* the narrator, who actually talked with him in his old age. He is furthermore a paradigmatic character: a model workman, not an average man, but one of those rare persons reared 'here and there in every generation of our peasant artisans' (ch. 19). Since Adam is also morally impeccable, there is no need for the narrator to supply the analysis and evaluation she does for Arthur; nor need she bring to the surface Adam's beliefs. He articulates them himself, and whenever he does, it is clear that he is a spokesman for the narrator's own views on such key subjects as the terrible consequences of our deeds; the value of religion residing in feeling and practical activity rather than in doctrines; the positive value of suffering and sad experience; and its close connection with the power of loving.

Dinah Morris is also a spokesperson for the last of these concerns. But before considering her character/characterisation, it is well to remind oneself of what is too often overlooked in connection with *Adam Bede*: that the novel is as much a study of first love as it is of the later love that is linked to sorrow. There is a predominantly sober colouring in the novel, but there is early freshness as well. When, near the end, Adam wonders at the strength and sweetness of his new love for Dinah, the narrator is prompted to wonder 'How is it that the poets have said so many fine things about our first love, so few about our later love?' (ch. 51). It is puzzling that the question would even be posed, for the narrator had already implicitly answered it earlier in the novel in three remarkable passages of generalisation.

The first is the most high-pitched and conventional in its tropes, and the one most out of place in the landlocked rural world of *Adam Bede*. In chapter 3 the love of Seth Bede for Dinah is said to be 'hardly distinguishable from religious feeling'. Like 'autumn sunsets, or pillared vistas, or calm majestic statues, or Beethoven symphonies', the emotions of first love bring with them 'the consciousness that they are mere waves and ripples in an unfathomable ocean of love and beauty'. The second passage, in chapter 12, which generalises on Arthur's burgeoning feelings for Hetty, is more down to earth; but it is still rather too conventional in its comparison of the 'wondering rapture' of early love to that of a bud first opening to the morning; too effusive in its image of 'two brooklets that ask for nothing but to entwine themselves and ripple with ever-interlacing curves in the leafiest hiding-places'; and even bizarre in its figure of 'young unfurrowed souls [rolling] to meet each other like two velvet peaches that touch softly and are at rest'.

But the third passage is superlative – the foremost example in *Adam Bede* of how ravishing the *sententiae* of the George Eliot narrator can be, particularly in the early novels. The scene is the garden of the Hall Farm where Adam has gone to meet Hetty and help her gather currants. As he watches her, his heart fills:

It was to Adam the time that a man can least forget in after-life – the time when he believes that the first woman he has ever loved betrays by a slight something . . . that she is at least beginning to love him in return. The sign is so slight . . . yet it seems to have changed his whole being, to have merged an uneasy yearning into a delicious unconsciousness of everything but the present moment. So much of our early gladness vanishes utterly from our memory: we can never recall the joy with which we laid our heads on our mother's bosom or rode on our father's back in childhood; doubtless that joy is wrought up into our nature, as the sunlight of long-past mornings is wrought up in the soft mellowness of the apricot; but it is gone for ever from our imagination, and we can only *believe* in the joy of childhood. But the first glad moment in our first love is a vision which returns to us to the last, and brings with it a thrill of feeling intense and special as the recurrent sensation of a sweet odour breathed in a far-off hour of happiness.

(ch. 20)

One of the felicities of this passage is that its images are not conventional or imported, but drawn from the very garden where Adam is standing; the chosen fruit is not the more literary peach or apple but the unsung apricot; and images drawn from the more intimate and involving senses of touch and smell replace visual and auditory images. Another is its richness of implication. The romantic intensities of childhood are acknowledged but are said largely to vanish from memory with the result that the rememberable gladness of first love comes to fill the space of that lost radiance. Yet the passage does not gainsay, so much as subtly reformulate, the Wordsworthian view that in later life the soul remembers *how* it felt (but not *what* it felt) during intense childhood experiences and thus retains what in the second book of the *Prelude* is called 'an obscure sense / Of possible sublimity' that is the enabling condition of the later transporting experiences. No wonder, then, that like Wordsworth himself Marian Evans also found during her early creative years that her mind worked with 'the keenest sense of poetry' when it was in touch with the 'remotest past'.

Adam's later love is for Dinah Morris, who is an even more idealised character than he. In her 1856 review of *Rachel Gray* Marian had observed that in her experience of piety among the uneducated she had found no example of religious intensity 'which has no *brogue*'; and she had complained that the 'essentially beautiful' feelings of the title character exhibited themselves as abstract virtues and not 'as qualities belonging to an individual character, of mixed moral nature and uncultured intellect' (*Leader*, 5 January 1856, 19). Exactly the same complaint can be made concerning Dinah. Not only has she no *brogue*; her 'mellow treble tones' have 'a variety of modulation like that of a fine instrument touched with the unconscious skill of musical instinct' (ch. 2). The total absence of self-consciousness in Dinah's demeanour is another outward and visible sign of the fact that she has no ego. Dinah is wholly filled with the divine presence and the divine pity. The implications of this for her characterisation are serious. Since she has no centre of self there is nothing for the narrator's powers of psychological omniscience to work on. The only indications in the text that Dinah has the capacity for a sublunary emotional life are strictly outside ones: the involuntary blushes that colour her faint cheek whenever she is near Adam.

The blood also rushes to Adam's face when his mother suggests

that he ask Dinah to marry him, advice that ultimately leads to
'The Meeting on the Hill' in chapter 54 and the coming together of
Adam and Dinah, never more to part. Henry James is not alone in
having expressed dissatisfaction with this union. The story should
have ended, he urged, 'with Hetty's execution, or even with her
reprieve'; Adam should have been left to his grief; and Dinah 'to
the enjoyment of that distinguished celibacy for which she was so
well suited'. In any event, thought James, their possible future
together was 'matter for a new story'.[7] It is difficult to agree with
this line of thinking. *Adam Bede* would surely have been incomplete
without an exemplification of later love – the love of which sorrow
and sad experience are essential constituents – to balance the
evocations of first love. Moreover, the exemplification is finely
realised. One key to its power and convincingness lies precisely in
its eschewal of psychological omniscience. When Adam tells Dinah
in chapter 52 that 'I love you with my whole heart and soul. I love
you next to God who made me', a strictly outside point of view is
used to communicate her reaction: her lips become as pale as her
cheeks, her hands cold as death and she trembles violently.
Another key is that there are no fine things said about this love by
the narrator, no generalisations, no imagery of natural fecundity,
pillared vistas, immeasurable ocean or mingling brooklets. There is
rather the bare hill outside the 'little grey, desolate looking hamlet'
of Sloman's End, a place of 'assured loneliness' where, as the
afternoon shadows lengthen and the lights grow softer, Adam
chooses to wait for Dinah 'away from all eyes – no house, no cattle,
not even a nibbling sheep near – no presence but the still lights and
shadows, and the great embracing sky' (ch. 54). And when they
are joined in marriage the following month, it is on a rimy morning
in late November.

There is much more in *Adam Bede* than characterisation and
sententiae, and a wider lens is needed to bring into focus the
aspect of the novel that is an unqualified success: its depiction of a
world. Narratorial gaucheries, unsubtle characterisation and dogmatic insistence count for little next to the fullness and vividness of
the picture of a rural community in the Midlands at the turn of the
eighteenth century. The representation includes the descriptions
of the natural world that Proust admired; such fully detailed
pictures as Dinah preaching on the village green, Bartle Massey's
night school, and parishioners conversing outside the Hayslope
church before and after the Sunday service; and such characters as

old Kester Bale, the farm worker whose forte was thatching and who would walk out of his way on a Sunday to admire his own work on the beehive ricks, and of course Mrs Poyser, whom Victorian and later readers have delighted in because of her sharp tongue, but whose utterance is never more memorable than in her comment on her aged father-in-law: 'Ah, I often think it's wi' th' old folks as it is wi' the babbies; they're satisfied wi' looking, no matter what they're looking at. It's God A'mighty's way o' quietening 'em, I reckon, afore they go to sleep' (ch. 18).

Silas Marner is a more slender and shapely work than *Adam Bede*, and a more finely calculated one. The first point made by R.H. Hutton in his review was that its 'conception is as fine as the execution is marvellous'. And if the more limited scope did not permit it to approach the tragic power of parts of *Adam Bede*, the shorter novel was a 'more perfect whole', with a 'more unique and subtle' plot. Hutton went on to remark on another striking feature of the work: 'the strong intellectual impress which the author contrives to give to a story of which the main elements are altogether unintellectual, without the smallest injury to the veri-similitude of the tale'. He gave as an example the splendid scene in the Rainbow tavern, during which, as the village butcher, farrier, tailor and parish clerk, wheelwright, and mole catcher converse in a seemingly desultory way, 'a faint shadow of the intellectual phases of "modern thought" . . . begins to fall on the discussion' (*CH*, 175–7). And Hutton could just as well have cited the scene between Silas and Dolly Winthrop in chapter 16. While the conver-sation at the Rainbow touches on epistemological questions con-cerning the difficulty of distinguishing subjective and objective, the relation of substance to form and in which of the two meaning could be said to reside, and the ability of the human mind to apprehend apparitions, the subject of the conversation in chapter 16 concerns providential belief and the problem of evil. What Dolly tells Silas in her homely idiom is both entirely in character and at the same time an epitome of a common Victorian response to the affliction of religious doubt. All that Dolly 'can be sure on', she says, is her trust in Providence:

> everything else is a big puzzle to me when I think on it. For there was the fever come and took off them as were full-growed, and left the helpless children; and there's the breaking o' limbs; and

them as 'ud do right and be sober have to suffer by them as are
contrairy – eh, there's trouble i' this world, and there's things as we
can niver make out the rights on. And all as we've got to do is to
trusten, Master Marner – to do the right thing as fur as we know,
and to trusten . . . I feel it i' my own inside as it must be so.

Hutton did not specify what was 'marvellous' about the execution of *Silas Marner*, but he hardly needed to. The most impressive
technical feature of this comparatively brief work is the skill with
which two different plots are alternated, counterpointed and made
mutually illuminating: the Silas Marner plot, the story of how a
common weaver, long estranged from his fellow men, is recalled to
life and to community through his love for a little child; and the
Godfrey Cass plot, which has no trace of the legendary about it (as
does the Marner plot), but rather studies the irresolute character of
a member of the gentry who in several particulars resembles
Arthur Donnithorne. The two plots are linked through several
comparable features: Silas is betrayed by his closest friend and
spiritual brother, William Dane, while Godfrey is deceived and
manipulated by his brother Dunstan; the former is an epitome of
what is narrow and perverted about the religious sect to which the
young Silas belonged; while the wholly corrupt Dunstan epitomises what his older brother is in danger of becoming. In his hour of
greatest need in Lantern Yard, Silas trusts in his God and looks to
the drawing of lots to clear him. In his troubles, Godfrey is equally
trusting in his deity, Chance, 'the god of all men who follow their
own devices', to save him from unpleasant consequences (ch. 9).
Both delusory beliefs are rooted in egotism rather than a wider,
other-regarding vision of human life and as such are the obverse of
Dolly Winthrop's belief in Providence. Finally, at the climax of the
novel, Silas and Godfrey come face to face in the presence of Eppie
as two contrasting versions of the 'natural' father.

If there is a serious flaw in the execution of *Silas Marner*, it occurs
in chapter 18 – the brief perfunctory scene in which Godfrey finally
tells his wife Nancy what he has long failed to muster the courage
to say: that he is the father of Eppie, the child whom sixteen years
before Silas took for his own while he remained silent. Earlier in
the novel the twistings of Godfrey's conscience and the pattern of
his habitual indecision had been detailed; and the previous chapter
had offered an extended inside view of Nancy that summarised
her fifteen years of marriage, registered her perception that the

lack of children was the one privation to which her husband could not be reconciled, and finely analysed the code of conduct and processes of thought that had led her to the view that adoption of children was against the will of Providence. But in chapter 18 no inside view is offered of either husband or wife. One learns nothing about the psychological circumstances that have led Godfrey to break his long silence, nor about any apprehensions he might have had concerning his wife's reaction. And Nancy's response to the news is registered solely through external notation. There is not a scintilla of information concerning her response to the revelation that her husband had been previously married and had fathered a child.

One suspects that the reason for the perfunctoriness of this chapter is a combination of authorial impatience to get to the climactic confrontation scene between the two fathers and the calculation that a fuller treatment of the Godfrey–Nancy interaction would have led to an imbalance in the plots. Whatever the reasons, chapter 19 is all that it should be and contains, *inter alia*, an acuity of psychological notation concerning Godfrey and Nancy that does much to compensate for its absence in the previous chapter. In this splendid scene Godfrey's nemesis – Eppie's refusal to change her station in life – is shown to be deserved not only because of his past irresolution and dependence on Chance but also because of a certain spot of commonness (to borrow a phrase from *Middlemarch*) linked to his privileged social position. In thinking that he has a right to Eppie, whose presence in his life would make his married happiness complete, Godfrey betrays a degree of unreflecting egotism not untypical of the way it is 'with all men and women who reach middle age without the clear perception that life never *can* be thoroughly joyous: under the vague dulness of the grey hours, dissatisfaction seeks a definite object, and finds it in the privation of an untried good' (ch. 17).

Husband and wife explain that they intend to make a lady of Eppie (it is what Hetty Sorrell hoped that Arthur Donnithorne would do for her). When Eppie replies that she can't leave her father and couldn't give up 'the folks I've been used to', Godfrey feels an irritation made inevitable by his inability 'to enter with lively appreciation into other people's feelings'; and his utterance is not unmixed with anger when he urges his 'natural claim . . . that must stand before every other'. Even Nancy shows a similar spot of commonness connected with her 'plenteous circumstances and the privileges of "respectability"'. Despite the 'acute sensibility of her own affections', her sympathies are insufficiently extended to enable her to enter 'into the pleasures which early nurture and habit connect with all the little aims and efforts of the poor who are born poor'.

While the two plots of which *Silas Marner* is composed are roughly equal quantitatively, it is the Marner plot that is qualitatively superior. The key to the distinction of this half of the novel is found in extensive use of psychological omniscience on what would seem to be a most unpromising subject – an unlettered linen weaver of pinched background and narrow notions whose consciousness has been further shrivelled as a result of betrayal and subsequent estrangement from human or natural comforters. The decision to apply the fullness of narratorial omniscience to this subject was the key creative decision taken by Marian Evans. In her February 1861 letter to her publisher explaining her intention (setting 'in a strong light the remedial influences of pure, natural human relations'), she observed that 'since William Wordsworth is dead', she could imagine that few would be interested in such an endeavour. Presumably with Wordsworthian precedents in mind, she had felt that her subject – the linen weaver remembered from childhood that had come to her 'as a sort of legendary tale' – 'would have lent itself best to metrical rather than prose fiction'. But as her mind dwelt upon the subject, she became 'inclined to a more realistic treatment' (*L*, iii, 382).

The treatment begins in chapter 1 with the flashback to Silas' youth and continues through the extended inside view in the following chapter, which details the growing desiccation of his consciousness after the move to Raveloe. In *Eugénie Grandet* Balzac's narrator observes that a miser's life is built on the rock of his egotism and manifested in feelings of vanity and self-interest. But Marner's growing obsession with his gold is rather shown to be the outer sign of an inward emptiness and aridity, and is said to be similar to the inner shrinking 'undergone by wiser men, when they have been cut off from faith and love'. By the present time of the narrative, Marner's life has become 'like a rivulet that has sunk far down from the grassy fringe of its old breadth into a little shivering thread, that cuts a groove for itself in the barren sand'.

The water begins to rise again through a seemingly providential dispensation: Silas' gold is stolen and its place taken by the golden-haired Eppie. But in a striking passage of precise notation at the end of chapter 12, the sudden beginnings of inner change in Silas are shown to be psychologically grounded in his past life. Eppie's little round form and shabby clothing remind him of his lost little sister, and under the double pressure of 'inexplicable surprise [finding Eppie on his hearth] and a hurrying influx of memories' Silas begins to experience sympathetic vibrations and intimations of a higher power:

> there was a vision of the old home and the old streets leading to Lantern Yard – and within that vision another, of the thoughts which had been present with him in those far-off scenes. The thoughts were strange to him now, like old friendships impossible to revive; and yet he had a dreamy feeling that this child was somehow a message come to him from that far-off life: it stirred fibres that had never been moved in Raveloe – old quiverings of tenderness – old impressions of awe at the presentiment of some Power presiding over his life; for his imagination had not yet extricated itself from the sense of mystery in the child's sudden presence, and had formed no conjectures of ordinary natural means by which the event could have been brought about.

At this moment Silas seems more than anything else a figure of the 'George Eliot' novelist with his millet seeds of early memories, his dreamy feeling and the sudden access of power. Certainly the trigger of the regeneration of Silas Marner is no more or less miraculous than was the conception of *Silas Marner*. And in both there is a subsequent inclining to more realistic treatment, as Silas' care for Eppie leads him out into the community, creating fresh links between his life and the life of others, sending him back to the natural world to look for the medicinal herbs that his mother had long ago taught him to use, and leading him to endorse the providential vision of Dolly Winthrop: 'There's good i' this world – I've a feeling o' that now; and it makes a man feel as there's a good more nor he can see . . . there's dealings with us – there's dealings' (ch. 16).

Like *Adam Bede, Silas Marner* ends with a wedding – another of those customary rituals that serve to foster the sense of community and of continuity in time. But there is no marriage at the end of *The Mill on the Floss*, the novel that came between these two recreations of past rural life. In her second novel, Marian Evans took as her social–historical subject not late eighteenth-century village life but the society of a nineteenth-century town from which the central character becomes alienated because of the uncontrollable intensities of her divided nature.

5

The Woman Question /
The Mill on the Floss (1860)

> What was it, he wondered, that made Maggie's dark eyes re-
> mind him of the the stories about princesses being turned into
> animals? . . . . . . I think it was that her eyes were full of unsatis-
> fied intelligence, and unsatisfied, beseeching affection.
>
> *The Mill on the Floss*

Two features of the early fiction of Marian Evans have been
hitherto unmentioned: the employment of a male pseudonym, and
the masculine self-references of the narrator. There are several
examples of the latter in *Scenes of Clerical Life*: 'Let me discover that
the lovely Phoebe thinks my squint intolerable', we hear on one
occasion, 'and I shall never be able to fix her blandly with my
disengaged eye again'; and in another place, the narrator recalls
that 'he' had once blushed when he thought he was being laughed
at 'because I was appearing in coat-tails for the first time' (*Amos
Barton*, ch. 2; *Janet's Repentance*, ch. 2). After *The Mill on the Floss*,
the gender-specific references stopped, and in time it became
well-known that the author of the George Eliot novels was a
woman. But most readers and reviewers of the *Scenes* and *Adam
Bede* were not as perceptive as Dickens, who immediately guessed
from internal evidence that their author was a woman.

Marian explained that she employed a *nom de plume* because it
'secures all the advantages without the disagreeables of reputation'
(*L*, ii, 292). She hardly needed to add that the principal disagree-
able had to do with her disreputable private life. As a Mrs O. Jones
remarked at a dinner party attended by Barbara Leigh Smith, who
reported the comment to Marian: *Adam Bede* 'could not have
succeeded if it had been known as hers; *every newspaper critic would
have written against it*' (*L*, iii, 103). But why was a male pseudonym
chosen and masculine characteristics indicated? Part of the answer
is familiarity: Marian had earlier used a male persona in her

Westminster Review articles. Her reasons for doing so are clear from a comment she made on one of them: 'The article appears to have produced a strong impression, and that impression would be a little counteracted if the author were known to be a *woman*' (*L*, ii, 218). The same prudential consideration applied to novels. As Lewes explained to Barbara: 'the object of anonymity was to get [*Adam Bede*] judged on its own merits, and not prejudged as the work of a woman, or of a particular woman'. He correctly remembered that when Charlotte Brontë's *Jane Eyre*, published in 1847 under the androgynous pseudonym of Currer Bell, was finally known to be by a woman, the tone of the reviews noticeably changed (*L*, iii, 106; ii, 506).

This tendency to prejudgement on the part of male reviewers largely accounts for the widespread employment of male or androgynous pen names by women novelists in the period between 1840 and 1880, during which increasing numbers of their productions appeared on the literary scene. As early as 1852, Lewes had commented on this proliferation in a breezy piece in the *Westminster* entitled 'The Lady Novelists'. Its significance, he thought, was 'not lightly to be passed over. It touches both society and literature'. Women had different 'organizations' than men and consequently different experiences, which would in turn lead to the introduction of a new element into literature. Roughly speaking, the female had a predominantly emotional organisation (that of the male was predominantly intellectual) and 'by her greater affectionateness, her greater range and depth of emotional experience' woman was 'well fitted to give expression to the emotional facts of life'. But hitherto, with some exceptions, of which Jane Austen and George Sand were the most illustrious, the literature of women had 'fallen short of its function' because it was too imitative of the literature of men. Prose fiction was the department of literature for which women were best adapted: 'the domestic experiences which form the bulk of woman's knowledge find an appropriate form in novels . . . The joys and sorrows of affection, the incidents of domestic life, the aspirations and fluctuations of emotional life, assume typical forms in the novel' (*WR*, 58 [1852], 129–33).

It is not surprising that Marian Evans, who was editing the *Westminster* when Lewes's article appeared, largely agreed with his views, though the authority and penetration with which she addresses the subject are markedly different from Lewes' more superficial discourse. For Marian, it was 'an immense mistake to maintain that there is no sex in literature'. In her view, science had no sex because it involved only the knowing and reasoning powers; but 'in art and literature, which imply the action of the entire being . . . woman has something specific to contribute'. This was evident in the field of prose fiction; women had already produced 'novels not only fine, but among the very finest; – novels, too, that have a precious speciality, lying quite apart from masculine aptitudes and experience'. But far too many inferior novels were being published by women: no educational restrictions 'shut women out from the materials of fiction, and there is no species of art which is so free from rigid requirements. Like crystalline masses, it may take any form and yet be beautiful'. But these very conditions had become part of the problem. The absence of rigid requirement constituted 'the fatal seduction of novel-writing to incompetent women' who lacked 'those moral qualities that contribute to literary excellence – patient diligence, a sense of the responsibility involved in publication, and an appreciation of the sacredness of the writer's art' (*Essays*, 53, 324, 323). In short, 'Women have not to prove that they can be emotional, and rhapsodic, and spiritualistic; every one believes that already. They have to prove that they are capable of accurate thought, severe study, and continuous self-command' (*WR*, 66 [1856], 578).

It is clear from these opinions and from her employment of the male pseudonym that while Marian regarded the female sensibility as distinctive, she wished to have fiction by women judged by standards similar, if not identical, to that produced by males. Until recently, the same criteria by and large prevailed in critical discourse on the George Eliot novels. For example, as George Levine has noted, the mid-twentieth-century revaluation of the novels 'came primarily from critics who saw her in the context of dominant traditions of literary history and criticism. Comparisons tended not to be with Mrs. Gaskell or Charlotte Brontë, but with Dickens, James and Lawrence'.[1] In the last twenty years, however, feminist literary criticism has introduced categories of sex and gender into the discussions of the fiction of Marian Evans.

One of the problems encountered by feminist commentators is that by either Victorian or contemporary criteria Marian was not a feminist and did not espouse a feminist ideology. She was certainly concerned with the intellectual culture of women and with the 'unjust laws and artificial restrictions' that hindered the full development of the possibilities of woman's nature. But the point of view in the following passage from an 1855 review article on Margaret Fuller and Mary Wollstonecraft can hardly be called *engagé* (least of all in its closing citation of Tennyson's *Princess*):

> On one side we hear that woman's position can never be improved until women themselves are better; and, on the other, that women can never become better until their position is improved – until the laws are made more just, and a wider field opened to feminine activity. But we constantly hear the same difficulty stated about the human race in general. There is a perpetual action and reaction between individuals and institutions; we must try to mend both by little and little – the only way in which human things can be mended. Unfortunately, many overzealous champions of women assert their actual equality with men – nay, even their moral superiority to men – as a ground for their release from oppressive laws and restrictions. They lose strength immensely by this false position. If it were true, then there would be a case in which slavery and ignorance nourished virtue, and so far we should have an argument for the continuance of bondage. But we want freedom and culture for woman, because subjection and ignorance have debased her, and with her, Man; for –
> If she be small, slight-natured, miserable,
> How shall men grow?
>
> (*Essays*, 200, 205)

Marian remained aloof from the women's rights agitations of the 1860s and 1870s despite the active involvement in the struggle of some of her closest friends. As early as 1857, she commented as follows on Charles Bray's pamphlet *The Industrial Employment of Women* and Barbara Leigh Smith's *Women and Work*:

> 'Conscience goes to the hammering in of nails' is my Gospel. There can be no harm in preaching *that* to women, at any rate. But I should be sorry to undertake any more specific enunciation of doctrine on a question so entangled as the 'Woman Question.' The part of the Epicurean gods is always an easy one; but because I prefer it so strongly myself, I the more highly venerate those who are struggling in the thick of the contest.
>
> (*L*, ii, 396)

Part of the reason for Marian's above-the-battle stance had to do with self-consciousness caused by her equivocal social position. There were many points concerning women that 'want being urged', she told Barbara in 1868: 'but they do not come well from me, and I never like to be quoted in any way on this subject' (*L*, iv, 425). But the opinions that she did express to her correspondents are perfectly consistent with her essentially conservative social and moral views and with the sensibility and the aesthetic aims that inform her fiction.

In 1867 she wrote to John Morley that she would 'certainly not oppose any plan which held out any reasonable prospect of tending to establish as far as possible an equivalence of advantage for the two sexes, as to education and the possibilities of free development'. But her principal interest was in more fundamental considerations:

> as a fact of mere zoological evolution, woman seems to me to have the worse share in existence. But for that very reason I would the more contend that in the moral evolution we have 'an art which does mend nature' – an art which 'itself is nature.' It is the function of love in the largest sense, to mitigate the harshness of all fatalities. And in the thorough recognition of that worse share, I think there is a basis for a sublimer resignation in woman and a more regenerating tenderness in man.
>
>   . . . The one conviction on the matter which I hold with some tenacity is, that through all transitions the goal towards which we are proceeding is a more clearly discerned distinctness of function (allowing always for exceptional cases of individual organization) with as near an approach to equivalence of good for woman and for man as can be secured by the effort of growing moral force to lighten the pressure of hard non-moral outward conditions.
>
> (*L*, viii, 402–3)

From this perspective, canvassing on the Women's Suffrage question appeared of little moment. 'Why', Marian asked Sara Hennell in 1867, 'should you burthen yourself in that way, for such an extremely doubtful good?' (*L*, iv, 390). She was more sympathetic to the movement for women's education and donated £50 towards the establishment of Girton, a Cambridge college for women. But this interest was not so much in the improvement of women *per se* as in a more general societal amelioration. As she wrote in 1868:

What I should like to be sure of as a result of higher education for women – a result that will come to pass over my grave – is, their recognition of the great amount of social unproductive labour which needs to be done by women, and which is now either not done at all or done wretchedly.

No good can come to women, more than to any class of male mortals, while each aims at doing the highest kind of work, which ought rather to be held in sanctity as what only the few can do well. I believe – and I want it to be well shown – that a more thorough education will tend to do away with the odious vulgarity of our notions about functions and employment, and to propagate the true gospel that the deepest disgrace is to insist on doing work for which we are unfit – to do work of any sort badly.

(*L*, iv, 425)

As with her earlier comments about conscience going to the hammering in of nails, this is the gospel according to Robert Evans, Adam Bede and Caleb Garth in *Middlemarch*, not the gospel according to John Stuart Mill, whose *Subjection of Women* was published the following year.

It is similarly difficult to find any of Mill's radical thinking in Marian's views on marriage, the institution of which came under increasing attack in the 1860s and 1870s. It is important to remember that Marian always regarded her union with Lewes as a marriage (though not of course a legally sanctioned one) entailing solemn responsibilities. She was much vexed when Bessie Parkes continued to address letters to 'Miss Evans' after their cohabitation had begun, and insisted on being addressed as Mrs Lewes. This and other biographical evidence make it plain that Marian Evans was not a rebel against the institution of marriage but rather, as Patricia Thomson put it, 'an unwilling victim of [the] legal anomalies' of Victorian society.[2] Moreover, with one exception it is not possible to find in Marian's creative work any serious interrogation of the institution of marriage; and the exception is one of the kind that proves the rule.

Marian's dramatic poem 'Armgart' was written in 1870 and published the following year. Its schema is that of a number of nineteenth-century poems which oppose the Romantic quest of the aspiring central character – Byron's Manfred, Browning's Paracelsus, Arnold's Fausta (in his 'Resignation') – to the claims of the normal and everyday. In Marian's poem this schema is adapted to the exploration of questions concerning gender and marriage. Armgart is a singer with an exceptional gift; her voice is even compared to that of Orpheus in its rare combination of 'natural good' and transporting 'spiritual energy'. Each time Armgart sings, new channels seem opened allowing her auditors to 'hear heaven better'. But in the view of Graf Dornberg, who wants her for his wife, 'too much ambition has unwomaned' Armgart. 'A woman's rank', he says, 'Lies in the fulness of her womanhood: / Therein alone she is royal'. The aspiring singer replies that the same 'Nature' that gave her her voice 'gave me ambition too', as well as the 'sense transcendent' that enables her to savour her power over audiences and consequent renown. The Graf counters with the warning that her (female) ambition is not 'robust enough for this gross world' and urges that she be content to concentrate her power 'in home delights / Which penetrate and purify the world'. In offering marriage, he asks of her 'a great renunciation'. Her answer includes the observation that in being a husband he could be something else as well and why should not the same be true of her as a wife? Unless she finds a man who will honour and cherish her art and not simply tolerate it, she will 'live alone, and pour my pain / With passion into music'.

The peripeteia in the poem is sudden. In two brief scenes that take place a year later, Armgart is first reported to have a danger-ous throat infection and then found to have lost her singing voice – though not her speaking voice, as is clear from her operatic lamen-tations ('see a soul / Made keen by loss . . . Oh, I had meaning once / Like day and sweetest air. What am I now?'). In the long final scene of the poem, Armgart has to face up to the Graf's loss of interest in her: 'though he doesn't say so outright', as Kathleen Blake has observed, 'for Armgart to sacrifice her art is essential to her appeal' to him.[3] The notation is acute, but incidental to Arm-gart's struggle to face up to her reduced status in the world. The title of the book of her life, she says, is henceforth to be 'The Woman's Lot: a Tale of Everyday'; and she sees herself as 'Pris-oned in all the petty mimicries / Called woman's knowledge'. The terminology used in Marian's 1867 letter to John Morley fits Arm-gart's situation exactly. Once she is no longer an exceptional case of individual organisation, her woman's destiny becomes not the artistic sublime but a 'sublimer resignation'. Walpurga, her humble confidante, counsels a life of 'joy by negatives' and a 'new birth' to be achieved by putting off the old 'monstrous Self' that looked down on ordinary humanity and becoming 'levelled with the crowd'. At the end Armgart finally learns that 'true vision comes . . . with sorrow'; she resolves to move to the provinces and teach music in a small town.

Thus, while 'Armgart' does explore questions concerning gender and marriage, the interrogation is superseded by the more urgent thematic imperative of resignation. In any event, Armgart's orphic gifts make her unrepresentative of women in general and set her apart from the central female characters in the George Eliot novels, most if not all of which answer to the description of Esther Lyon in chapter 44 of *Felix Holt*: 'she was intensely of the feminine type, verging neither towards the saint nor the angel. She was a "fair divided excellence, whose fulness of perfection" must be in marriage'. In *Middlemarch*, for example, Dorothea Brooke initially has exalted spiritual ambitions; but by the end of the novel, she has found fulfilment and happiness in the unsung roles of mother and of wife and helpmate to the man she loves.

It is true that in *Felix Holt* and in *Middlemarch* the fulfilment-through-marriage plot is linked to what the final chapter of the latter calls 'the conditions of an imperfect social state'; and it is to Dorothea that the narrator is referring when she says that 'there is no creature whose inward being is so strong that it is not greatly determined by what lies outside it'. The narrator of *Felix Holt* is equally insistent on the point. In chapter 3 she observes that 'there is no private life which has not been determined by a wider public life', and later on is more specific as to how this rule applies to Esther Lyon: 'After all, she was a woman, and could not make her own lot. As she had once said to Felix, "A woman must choose meaner things, because only meaner things are offered to her." Her lot is made for her by the love she accepts' (ch. 43). But it is not the case that the George Eliot novels suggest that an improvement in social conditions will lead to a change in the locus where a woman's fulness of perfection is to be found. In the first edition of *Middlemarch*, the penultimate paragraph of its final chapter had specified the social conditions of the early 1830s against which Dorothea Brooke struggled and thereby left readers in the less restrictive conditions of the 1870s free to think that the lot of women might be changed by the removal of particular social impediments. But in later editions this passage was replaced by a more general reference to 'young and noble impulse struggling amidst the conditions of an imperfect social state', thereby suggesting a perennial rather than a remediable situation. As Marian put it in her letter to Morley, 'as a fact of mere zoological evolution' women had the worse share in existence; the harshness of their condition could be mitigated by love and/or by resignation, and it was hoped that ultimately a growing moral force would lighten 'the pressure of hard non-moral outward conditions'. But the disappearance of the pressure is not envisioned.

In the light of all this, it is no wonder that in the 1970s 'George Eliot' became, as Elizabeth Showalter has noted, 'the most difficult and controversial figure for feminist literary criticism'.[4] Marian Evans had established herself independently of her family, earned her own living, edited a journal, expressed advanced opinions in print, had a liaison with a married man, lived openly with him in defiance of convention, and attained both private happiness and vocational fulfilment through doing so. But none of this was ever reflected in the lives of her female characters. Just as Marian had lived through the Victorian crisis of belief but never made it the subject matter of her fiction, so too she lived the life of an emancipated woman but never wrote about it. Instead, her heroines either dwindled into wives or were forced to swallow the pills of renunciation and resignation.

Feminist animadversions were countered by other commentators, some of whom made the essential point that the differences between the life of Marian Evans and those of her central female characters were the consequence of her artistic purposes and fictional methods. One can nevertheless be made uneasy over the fact that while 'All self-sacrifice is good', as she had remarked of *Jane Eyre*, Marian seemed to regard this as being particularly the case for women. It is also hard to forget that when she decided to live openly with Lewes in 1854, she acted, as Lord Acton pointed out, 'in contradiction to that which was the dominant and enduring spirit of her own work'.[5] It would seem that while all self-sacrifice is good, there are some things that are better, even for a woman. It is hard not to think that Marian Evans was herself uneasy about these matters and that this ambivalence is reflected in the discontinuities of her second novel, the central character of which wishes she 'could make myself a world outside [loving], as men do', but cannot (ch. 46).

The Mill on the Floss is Marian's most autobiographical novel. The setting of its first two-thirds is unmistakeably the Warwickshire of her childhood; and the early life of Maggie Tulliver and her older brother Tom resembles that of Marian and her older brother Isaac. One might even say of the novel that it is the book Marian wrote because it 'was impossible for her to write an autobiography'. Marian made this observation about herself in 1869 to Emily Davies, co-founder of Girton College, during a conversation that had turned to the subject of *The Mill on the Floss*. Her 'sole purpose' in writing the novel, she said on that occasion, 'was to show the conflict which is going on everywhere when the younger generation with its higher culture comes into collision with the older, and in which . . . so many young hearts make shipwreck far worse than Maggie'. She went on to say that in the novel 'everything is softened, as compared with real life', and that her own experience 'was worse' (*L*, viii, 465). But Marian did not specify in what ways her own experience was worse than that of Maggie – a judgement the grounds for which are by no means self-evident. Nor did she say whether this alleged 'softening' was calculated or inadvertent.

Certainly the world of *The Mill on the Floss* does not feel soft in comparison with that of *Adam Bede* and *Silas Marner*; just the opposite is the case. The dissimilarities were pointed up by E.S. Dallas at the beginning of his review in *The Times*. The characters in *Adam Bede* were all likeable and the 'general influence of the book was to reconcile us to human nature, to make us think better of our fellow men . . . to draw us nearer to each other by showing how completely we are one, and so to give us . . . the permanent good of an increased sympathy with our kind'. But the second George Eliot novel introduced 'a very different set of personages', the majority of whom were 'prosaic, selfish, nasty. We are launched into a world of pride, vain-glory, and hypocrisy, envy, hatred and malice, and all uncharitableness . . . we have the petty gossip and malignant slander of village worthies painted to the life . . . Everybody in this tale is repelling everybody, and life is in the strictest sense a battle' (*CH*, 132–3).

One essential difference between the two pictures is that the former describes a village community at an appreciable historical remove from the present, while the latter depicts a town society in the fourth decade of the nineteenth century. The narrator of *Adam Bede*, one may say, was a social historian depicting with a loving detail reminiscent of seventeenth-century Dutch painters a self-sufficient farming culture untouched by the industrial revolution. On the other hand, the narrator of *The Mill on the Floss* often resembles a social scientist observing the effects of hereditary conditions on an organism, and the latter's interaction with the 'oppressive narrowness' of its environment. Small details are important not only in making the depiction vivid but also because of their diagnostic value: 'In natural science', the narrator reports, 'there is nothing petty to the mind that has a large vision of relations, to which every single object suggests a vast sum of conditions. It is surely the same with the observation of human life' (ch. 30).

In his review Dallas had gone on to detail some of the unpleasant materials of which the novel was composed. When she read his review, Marian was taken aback:

> I have certainly fulfilled my intention very badly if I have made the Dodson honesty appear 'mean and uninteresting,' or made the payment of one's debts appear a contemptible virtue in comparison with any sort of 'Bohemian' qualities. So far as my own feeling and intention are concerned, no one class of persons or form of character is held up to reprobation or to exclusive admiration. Tom is painted with as much love and pity as Maggie, and I am so far from hating the Dodsons myself, that I am rather aghast to find them ticketed with such very ugly adjectives.
>
> (*L*, iii, 299)

What is most interesting about this disagreement between critic and author is that each has a point. Within the text of *The Mill on the Floss*, there are two different points of view from which the world of St Ogg's is viewed – the close-up and the distanced – and characters and customs can look very different depending on the perspective. One example is found in the depiction of the shared childhood experiences of Maggie and Tom. Most of the time when they are alone together, they wind up making each other unhappy; but when their sibling bond is the subject of the narrator's retrospective generalisations, a prelapsarian glow surrounds the time when brother and sister had 'clasped their little hands in love, and roamed the daisied fields together' (ch. 58).

While narratorial generalisation sometimes softens the picture, at other times the opposite is the case: the close-up showing is in soft focus, while the retrospective telling has a hard edge. This is particularly true in the case of the Dodson aunts and uncles. There is a good deal of genial flavour and good humour in the character sketches and copiously detailed scenes devoted to these characters. But all of the charm disappears from a distanced perspective in which the Dodsons and Tullivers appear 'emmet-like' and to be living 'a sordid life . . . the most prosaic form of human life [with] little trace of religion, still less of a distinctively Christian creed', and 'no standard beyond hereditary custom. You could not live among such people' (ch. 30). But even the distanced perspective made possible by temporal omniscience does not ensure consistent evaluation. Take, for example, the point concerning the payment of debts. In chapter 31, when the narrator begins a paragraph of generalisation concerning 'the narrow notions about debt, held by the old-fashioned Tullivers', one expects that another item in the catalogue of St Ogg's pettiness is about to be detailed. But by the end of the paragraph the irony is turned around and the probity of the Dodsons and Tullivers becomes a standard of integrity to which readers in the 1860s might have had trouble measuring up.

These narratorial discontinuities suggest that even as she entered her fifth decade, Marian Evans still had ambivalent feelings about her early experiences and the world in which she grew up. Other evidence is found in the life story of Maggie Tulliver, the novel's central character, and in the novel's catastrophic ending. Before proceeding to these subjects, however, one further aspect of Marian's reaction to E.S. Dallas' review needs to be considered. To put the matter bluntly: how could she ever have persuaded herself that Tom Tulliver was painted with as much love and pity as Maggie? One takes the point when Marian complains of another reviewer's attribution to her of a 'disdain for Tom, as if it were not *my* respect for Tom which infused itself into my reader – as if he could have respected Tom, if I had not painted him with respect' (*L*, iii, 397). Such critical presumption is quite properly rebuked by the author. But the presentation of Tom infuses qualities other than respect into readers.

At one point, the narrator describes the subject of her novel to be how the 'oppressive narrowness' of St Ogg's 'acted on the lives of Tom and Maggie'. Strictly speaking, this is the case; but surely it is experientially true for all readers of *The Mill on the Floss* that the novel is predominantly Maggie's, and Tom is the principal representative of the society that acts with such an oppressively negative force on her. In particular, Tom is the epitome of society's attitudes to gender. These attitudes are instanced in other characters as well: Mr Stelling, for example, who assures his pupil Tom that girls 'can pick up a little of everything . . . They've got a great deal of superficial cleverness; but they couldn't go far into anything. They're quick and shallow' (ch. 14). But it is Tom who does most of the talking concerning the deficiencies of Maggie's sex. And it is he who is the novel's dominant symbol of repressive male authority.

It may seem to be saying a lot for a young man with some sterling qualities, who toils for years to pay off his father's debts; but with reference to his sister Maggie and her deepest needs, Tom is a repulsive and terrifying figure. In chapter 5, when he discovers that she has forgotten to take care of his rabbits, he immediately tells her he doesn't love her and that he will not forget the episode. His masculine petulance in the scene involving the division of the jam puff is equally telling; so too his conduct when he dresses up as a soldier, terrifies Maggie by pointing a large sword at her, and begins to smile complacently while she trembles and begins to cry. Tom's boyish sense of justice is composed largely of 'his desire to punish': to 'hurt culprits as much as they deserve to be hurt' (chs. 10, 6). When he is older, it is Maggie who provides 'his strong self-asserting nature' with a culprit (ch. 25). When she observes that being a man means that he has the power to do something in the world, Tom replies: 'Then if you can do nothing, submit to those who can'. After all, 'a brother, who goes out into the world and mixes with men, necessarily knows better what is right and respectable for his sister than she can know herself' (chs. 37, 43). By the time he has reached his majority, Tom has been indelibly marked by 'the positive and negative qualities that create severity – strength of will, conscious rectitude of purpose, narrowness of imagination and intellect, great power of self-control, and a disposition to exert control over others'. When he sends Maggie from his door saying that 'I wash my hands of you for ever. You don't belong to me', he has become 'inexorable, unbending, unmodifiable' (chs. 51, 54). As for 'their early childish love in the time when they had clasped tiny fingers together' (ch. 56), Tom's adult feelings of repulsion from his sister are said to derive much of their intensity precisely from that early love.

This same early love is the bedrock of Maggie Tulliver's being. Of all her desires and longings, the most profound and abiding, that has its roots 'deeper than all change', is the 'perpetual yearning . . . to have no cloud between herself and Tom'. When

Philip Wakem complains that Maggie could never love him so much as she does her brother, she answers that 'the first thing I ever remember in my life is standing with Tom by the side of the Floss, while he held my hand: everything before that is dark to me' (chs. 51, 33). One might infer a correspondingly deep residual feeling in Marian Evans for her brother Isaac that would help account for the discrepancy between how she thought she had painted Tom and the dominant impression his portrait conveys. After all, in her 1869 'Brother and Sister' sonnets Marian describes in lovingly particularised detail the early days of sibling oneness that are only retrospectively alluded to in the novel, and that allow the poem to end with the poignant reflection that 'Were another childhood world my share, / I would be born a little sister there'. In any event, one result of the closeness between Maggie and Tom is that considerations of gender and male authority are always at least potentially present in the story of her development from a child into a young woman.

In chapter 42 the narrator remarks that if Maggie had been 'a thoroughly well-educated young lady, with a perfectly balanced mind [and] all the advantages of fortune, training and refined society', the reader 'would probably have known nothing about her: her life would have had so few vicissitudes that it could hardly have been written; for the happiest women, like the happiest nations, have no history'. One important consideration in connection with Maggie's history concerns the origin of these vicissitudes. In chapter 45 the narrator quotes one of the Novalis' axioms – 'character is destiny' – only to disagree with it. The tragedy of our lives, she says, 'is not created entirely from within', and character is not 'the whole of our destiny'. It is not the whole; but it may or may not be the dominant determinant; and it is by no means clear that the origin of Maggie's vicissitudes is less pathological than environmental or societal – despite what the narrator's remark about affluent and well-educated young ladies might be taken to suggest.

The first half of the novel contains a number of memorable vignettes and images of Maggie in the grip of moods and emotions that set her apart from others. Some of them certainly do call attention to the fact that she has been born into 'a gendered world where girls are driven by an intense need for male approval' and where Maggie's self-esteem is shown to be 'pitifully dependent on Tom's love', so much so that 'she will sacrifice any legitimate claim of her own personality to avoid rejection by him'.[6] But other aspects of Maggie's being seem to have their origin in nature rather than nurture. For example, her tendency to reverie and daydream – 'to sit down by the holly, or wander by the hedgerow, and fancy it was all different, refashioning her little world into just what she should like it to be' (ch. 6). Some examples of these low forms of expanded consciousness seem prompted by impingements from without; but two early glimpses of Maggie suggest an internal origin: the picture of the nine-year old child in chapter 1, standing outside Dorlcote Mill in the deepening gloom of a February afternoon 'rapt' in watching the rushing of the water and listening to the booming of the mill; and Mr Tulliver's remark in the next chapter concerning his daughter's tendency at the same age to forget what she has been asked to do 'an' perhaps . . . sit down on the floor i' the sunshine an' plait her hair an' sing to herself like a Bedlam creatur''.

Certainly it is not possible to assign an unequivocally environmental origin to the most important single component in Maggie's being: 'the need of being loved, the strongest need in poor Maggie's nature . . . this need of love – this hunger of the heart' (ch. 5). To Maggie herself, this need seems a generic constituent of certain women, 'the dark unhappy ones' whose stories do not have happy endings (ch. 36); and it is the principal reason why she is not wrong in thinking that she has had laid on her life 'the burthen of larger wants than others seemed to feel'. Maggie makes this reflection in chapter 32 just before she first opens the book of Thomas à Kempis that is to bring her 'knowledge of the irreversible laws within and without' and teach her the saving strengths of accepted sorrow and renunciation of worldly desires. Thomas' teaching sustains Maggie for some years, but by the time she has reached the post-pubescent age of sixteen it has begun to become clear that *The Imitation of Christ* cannot provide a permanent suppression of her deepest needs and resultant vicissitudes.

The outward and visible sign of the inefficacy is Maggie's physical being: her broad-chested figure which has the mould of early womanhood; 'her tall beauty crowned by the night of her massy hair' (ch. 48); her firm and rounded brown cheeks; her full red lips; and most of all her dark and liquid, deep and strange, eyes, to which attention is repeatedly called. The most often noted feature of both Dinah Morris and Dorothea Brooke is their voice – the least corporeal of all physical characteristics. But Maggie's synecdoche is her eyes – the quintessence of her physical attractiveness and the window of the being within. In the hazel eyes of Lucy Deane is seen an 'ever-present sunny benignity, in which the momentary harmless flashes of personal vanity are quite lost' (ch. 40). But in her cousin Maggie's eyes are seen 'eager passionate longings', 'wide hopeless yearning', and 'the rising again of her innate delight in admiration and love' (chs. 25, 32, 33).

It is to her eyes more than anything else that Philip Wakem is drawn; and it is through her developing relationship with him that Maggie's vows of renunciation are first tested. Eventually, Maggie allows herself to become engaged to Philip and had circumstances been otherwise would presumably have married him, thereby providing, as Lucy Deane puts it, 'a pretty ending to all my poor, poor Maggie's troubles' (ch. 42). It is not at all apparent, however, that this union would have been wholesome. The young D.H. Lawrence certainly didn't think so. According to Jessie Chambers, he 'adored' *The Mill on the Floss*, and Maggie Tulliver was his favourite heroine. But Lawrence 'always declared that George Eliot had "gone and spoilt it halfway through." He could not forgive the marriage [sic] of the vital Maggie Tulliver to the cripple Philip. He used to say: "It was wrong, wrong. She should never have made her do it"'.[7] It is hard not to sympathise with Lawrence's response. There is nothing in Philip Wakem to complement Maggie's vibrant physical being or satisfy her passionate nature. The love that she feels for Philip, like that for her brother, has its origin not in passion but in the past; it is a 'tranquil, tender affection . . . with its root deep down in her childhood' (ch. 46).

The claims of the present – the warm enchanted present from which the past and future are excluded – are represented by the handsome Stephen Guest, to whom Maggie's passionate nature irresistibly responds. A number of commentators from Swinburne to F.R. Leavis have had difficulty with Maggie's passion for Stephen and have regarded the latter as a serious flaw in the novel. An excellent corrective to this view is that of William Myers, who identifies Stephen as a representative of the new national economic and intellectual life of Britain that has begun to make its presence felt in the long-stagnant provincial culture of St Ogg's. 'He *is* shallow, egotistical and naively self-approving'; but he is not a coxcomb, and he does speak out sincerely 'in defence of an ethic of honesty and spontaneity in personal relations which the obliteration of Christian norms and sanctions would appear to justify'.[8]

But with reference to the main point of critical concern, which is not Stephen *per se* but rather Maggie's relation to him, the best commentator is Marian Evans herself. In refutation of Bulwer-Lytton's opinion that Maggie's indulgence of her passion was 'a treachery and a meanness according to the Ethics of Art', she replied:

> Maggie's position towards Stephen . . . is too vital a part of my whole conception and purpose for me to be converted to the condemnation of it. If I am wrong there – if I did not really know what my heroine would feel and do under the circumstances in which I deliberately placed her, I ought not to have written this book at all, but quite a different book, if any. If the ethics of art do not admit the truthful presentation of a character essentially noble but liable to great error – error that is anguish to its own nobleness – *then*, it seems to me, the ethics of art are too narrow, and must be widened to correspond with a widening psychology.
>
> (*L*, iii, 317–18)

The single aspect of this self-defence that gives one pause is the phrase concerning Maggie's liability to great error, which seems as inapposite as the narrator's references to Maggie's 'vanity' in chapter 48 and two chapters earlier to the 'vanity or other egoistic excitability of her nature'. Certainly there is egotism in Maggie in the sense of a tumultuous preoccupation with her personal lot; moreover, a certain degree of ego is a prerequisite for passionate love. But where is the vanity? Certainly not in Maggie's eyes. These asides strike false notes in the closing section of *The Mill on the Floss*, which powerfully displays the conflicting imperatives in Maggie's being: the passionate longings that can only be satisfied in the present, and the memories of early affections that are, as Maggie tells Stephen, 'the most sacred ties that can ever be formed on earth. If the past is not to bind us, where can duty lie. We should have no law but the inclination of the moment' (ch. 53).

Maggie cannot live without the past; but in the closing chapters of her novel she does not seem capable of living without present love either. A measure of the extremity of her plight is that none of the great sustaining positives in the George Eliot canon is able to reconcile the opposing currents of her being: not the 'bond of loving fellowship . . . which is the gift of sorrow' (ch. 20); not the doctrine of renunciation found in Thomas à Kempis; not the mitigation of an imputed egotism through the recognition of an equivalent centre of self in others; not the redeeming power of one human being's effect on another; not the ties of the past; and not the moral imperative of duty.

The only resolution for Maggie's vicissitudes is the catastrophic flood in which she and Tom are reunited in a supreme moment of fulfilment before they die in each other's arms. As Henry Crabb Robinson, one of the first readers of the novel, put it: 'a natural event determines the fate of the parties, and no act of theirs. A sad fault'.[9] Of the many subsequent commentators who have complained of the novel's ending, Barbara Hardy is particularly harsh in her condemnation of a 'solution by fantasy', an act of 'bad faith that contrasts so strongly with the authenticity of everything that comes before'.[10] I do not myself share this view and have elsewhere tried to change received opinion by suggesting that the providential dispensation at the novel's close be assigned to Maggie's visionary reverie rather than to authorial fantasy. But what there should be no disagreement over is that its ending is not the only indication in *The Mill on the Floss* of the difficulty Marian Evans had in resolving the conflicting emotions that energise her most autobiographical novel; and that this continuing quarrel with herself includes questions concerning the fate of passionate women, who cannot live without love, in a male-dominated society.

6

The 1860s / *Romola* (1863) and *The Spanish Gypsy* (1868)

The sleepless sense that a new code of duty and motive needed to be restored in the midst of the void left by lost sanctions and banished hopes never ceased to stimulate her faculties and to oppress her spirits.

Lord Acton

The publication of *Silas Marner* in 1861 brought Marian further critical acclaim and even more gratifying sales figures than those for her previous books. Only four years after *Scenes of Clerical Life* 'George Eliot' was established as one of the foremost novelists of the day and the creator of a distinctive fictional world with a distinctive *apport*. In Virginia Woolf's memorable formulation: 'Over them all broods a certain romance, the only romance that George Eliot allowed herself – the romance of the past'. But as Woolf went on to observe, 'the mist of recollection gradually withdraws'.[1] Marian's six subsequent books are different from their predecessors in subject, form and aesthetic preoccupation; and their sources – their germs or millet seeds – are not found in her early experience. It is true that two of her later novels are set in 'Loamshire' in the early 1830s; but neither *Felix Holt* nor *Middlemarch* simply offers the faithful representing of commonplace things. The former is a political novel with a tract-for-the-times dimension; while the latter, subtitled 'a study of provincial life', is less the *étude* of a genre painter than the *oeuvre* of a social scientist. This appreciable divide between the early and later works needs to be accounted for. The place to begin is with *Romola*, Marian's fourth novel, which she was later to say marked a turning point in her life: 'I began it a young woman, – I finished it an old woman' (Cross, ii, 273).

The germ of *Romola* was Lewes' suggestion, made during their stay in Florence in May 1860, that the city in the time of Savonarola afforded 'fine material for an historical romance'. Marian was immediately enthusiastic about the idea, even though it would be an ambitious project requiring 'a great deal of study and labour'. Lewes encouraged her to believe that she could do 'something in historical romance rather different in character from what has been done before'; and Blackwood was equally positive, telling Marian he expected she would 'return Historical Romance to its ancient popularity' (*L*, iii, 295, 307, 339, 340). By ancient he meant the period between Walter Scott, who had started the vogue for historical fiction, and the mid-1850s, when its popularity appeared to be waning despite the appearance during that decade of two such notable examples of the genre as Thackeray's *Henry Esmond* and Dickens' *A Tale of Two Cities*. Compared with the traditional village life of Hayslope or Raveloe, or with the stagnant culture of Milby or St Ogg's, the historical subject that Marian proposed to tackle was full of volatile and dramatic materials. The late 1400s in Florence were a time of political turmoil and cultural and religious conflict – a 'strange web of belief and unbelief', as it is called in the novel's 'Proem', 'of Epicurean levity and fetichistic dread; of pedantic impossible ethics uttered by rote, and crude passions acted out with childish impulsiveness; of inclination towards a self-indulgent paganism, and inevitable subjection to that human conscience which, in the unrest of a new growth, was filling the air with strange prophecies and presentiments'. Moreover, from the point of view of the would-be writer of historical romance, the ratio between individual actions and historical events was attractive. As Marian had noted in 1857: histories like that of the Reformation in southern Europe, 'which have their climax in persecution and martyrdom, and not in political revolution, necessarily treat chiefly of individual action and individual fates – the interest in the heroes of the conflict is not merged in the grand general results of the conflict' (*WR*, 67 [1857], 295).

But this distinction between foreground and background could by no means entirely alleviate the onerousness of the historical novelist's task. For Marian the task could 'only be justified by the rarest concurrence of acquirement with genius'. The ability to become familiar with 'the relics of an ancient period', and then, by the force of 'sympathetic divination, restore the missing notes in the "music of humanity," and reconstruct the fragments into a whole which will really bring the remote past nearer to us, and interpret it to our duller apprehension', was a 'form of imaginative power [that] must always be among the very rarest, because it demands as much accurate and minute knowledge as creative vigour' (*Essays*, 320–1). Certainly Marian made prodigious efforts to attain accurate and minute knowledge of her subject. Her background reading was enormous, and even seems to have bordered on the compulsive, as a comment of Lewes' suggests: 'At present she remains immovable in the conviction that she *can't* write the romance because she has not knowledge enough' (*L*, iii, 473–4).

As has long been recognised, one of the principal problems with the result of all Marian's labour is that *Romola* is crammed with far too much minute knowledge and circumstantial detail. This major aesthetic miscalculation could have been avoided if the example of her beloved Scott, 'the unequalled model of historical romancists', had been followed. In his 'Dedicatory Epistle' to *Ivanhoe*, Scott had spoken of 'the fair licence due to the author of a fictitious composition' of the type he had written. Of course this licence had to be confined within legitimate bounds. The writer must not plant cypress trees upon Inch Merrin, or Scottish firs among the ruins of Persepolis; and 'he must introduce nothing inconsistent with the manners of the age'. But too much antiquarian erudition was bad for an historical fiction. The writer should therefore try to occupy 'that extensive neutral ground, the large proportion, that is, of manners and sentiments which are common to us and to our ancestors' because they arise out of 'the principles of our common nature'. Their sources, and that of the passions, 'are generally the same in all ranks and conditions, all countries and ages'.[2] Since the point about essential similarities is forcefully made in the opening paragraph of *Romola* ('the same great needs, the same great loves and terrors . . . the broad sameness of the human lot, which never alters in the main headings of its history'), it is all the more surprising that the former is so completely forgotten.

What accounts for the disproportionate amount of factual material in *Romola*? Part of the answer lies in what may be called the Casaubon traits in Marian's character. In chapter 9 of *Middlemarch* that scholar remarks that 'for the achievement of any work regarded as an end there must be a prior exercise of many energies or acquired faculties of a secondary order, demanding patience'. But because he lacked the scholarly equivalent of creative vigour,

Casaubon substituted endless prolongation of the preliminary exercise for achievement of the work. Marian Evans did not do this; but the sheer amount of historical detail in her novel suggests a level of creative heat insufficient to allow for the distillation of the mash of acquired knowledge.

Another part of the answer is found in the letter Marian wrote to R.H. Hutton in Agusut 1863. In his review of *Romola*, Hutton had complained of 'the certainly somewhat unfortunate amplification of local gossip' in the first part of the novel: 'We do not care about the light Florentine buzz . . . Its allusions are half riddles, and its liveliness a blank to us' (*CH*, 205, 199). In her letter Marian did admit to a 'tendency to excess'; but she also believed that there was 'scarcely a phrase, an incident, an allusion, that did not gather its value to me from its supposed subservience to my main artistic objects'. It was, she continued

> the habit of my imagination to strive after as full a vision of the medium in which a character moves as of the character itself. The psychological causes which prompted me to give such details of Florentine life and history as I have given, are precisely the same as those which determined me in giving the details of English village life in 'Silas Marner,' or the 'Dodson' life, out of which were developed the destinies of poor Tom and Maggie.
>
> (*L*, iv, 97)

Here, one suspects, is the root of the miscalculation. The causes which prompted the fulness of detail may have been the same in *Romola* as in its predecessors, but the result was not. In the novel, one does not feel that 'the internal conditions and the external are related to each other as the organism and its medium' (to use a phrase from 'The Natural History of German Life'). It is not felt because the strong fabular and diagrammatic elements in *Romola* necessitate the stylisation and idealisation of the central characters to a degree far greater than anything found in Marian's earlier works. These features of the novel are unquestionably the result of a deliberate decision, though Marian does not seem to have sufficiently pondered the trade-offs involved. She spoke of *Romola* as being addressed to fewer readers than her previous books had been and of never intending that it should be 'as "popular" in the same sense as the others'. In another letter, she explains that the 'necessary idealization' she wanted her fourth novel to have 'could only be attained by adopting the clothing of the past'. And in a letter to Sara Hennell she agreed with her friend's having said that 'Romola is ideal . . . The various *strands* of thought I had to work out forced me into a more ideal treatment of Romola than I had foreseen at the outset – though the "Drifting Away" and the Village with the Plague [chapters 61 and 68] belonged to my earliest conception of the story and were by deliberate forecast adopted as romantic and symbolical elements' (*L*, iv, 49, 301, 103–4). It is elements such as these that carry much of the thematic freight in *Romola* and give the novel a fabular drift incompatible with realistic presentation. As George Levine has noted: the fabular elements 'function symbolically rather than naturalistically and . . . grow rather out of "*strands* of thought" than out of the inevitabilities of fully realized characters . . . the novel is controlled more by moral and intellectual preoccupations' than by the novelist's 'submission to the possibilities of her created world'. As a result, the progress of the title character was 'uninvolved in the wider life of the novel . . . the romance is never reconciled to the real'.[3]

The fact that *Romola* is comparatively inert, however, does not mean that it is unimpressive or without distinctive felicities. There are many striking points, though they are mainly found in the central characters themselves rather than in the idealised postures they are made to assume or in the medium on which Marian lavished so much care. The character study of Romola's husband is an example. It is true that Tito is a type of character that Marian had drawn before and would draw again, and that there are a number of over-insistent narratorial intrusions concerning the dreadful vitality of deeds. But Tito's portrait is distinguished by the quality of the notations marking the stages in his moral deterioration. At the outset, the imperfections of this charming young man seem slight – 'an innate love of reticence' that makes concealment easy and an 'unconquerable aversion to anything unpleasant' (chs. 9, 10). But these qualities have already led him not to pursue the search for his father, and to desire it to be the truth that he was dead. As a result, Tito's talent for concealment fast develops into something less morally neutral and stimulates his ingenuity to self-serving reflections ('What, looked at closely, was the end of all life but to extract the utmost sum of pleasure?' [ch. 11]). Outward signs of Tito's inner corruption soon become visible: 'The lines of the face were as soft as ever, the eyes as pellucid; but something was gone – something as indefinable as the changes in the morning twilight'. It is 'that change which comes from the final departure of moral youthfulness – from the distinct self-conscious adoption of a part in life' (ch. 22). The corruption inevitably contaminates his married life and he even comes to feel a certain repulsion from Romola, and to find comfort in Tessa's ignorant lovingness. His political machinations become more and more debased ('It was weakness only that was despised; power of any sort carried its own immunity'), and he is finally destroyed by the political game that had initially seemed to him simply 'an agreeable mingling of skill and chance' (ch. 57, 35).

The quality of the notations through which the course of Romola's feeling for Tito is traced is comparably high. But the finest scene involving the title character is one between her and Savonarola. I do not refer to their meeting in chapter 40 in which she plays Maggie Tulliver to his Thomas à Kempis, but rather to their interview in chapter 59. Through the Friar, Romola has come to believe in the Catholic Church as 'a living organism instinct with Divine power to bless and to curse'; but she feels 'her relation to the Church only through Savonarola; his moral force had been the only authority to which she had bowed' (ch. 55). That is to say, Romola is a proto-Protestant who doth prefer before all temples the upright heart and pure. When her faith in her mentor is shaken, the confrontation scene in chapter 59 ensues – the one place in the novel where the realistic and the fabular elements in the novel powerfully fuse.

The method used in the characterisation of Savonarola is significantly different from that used for Tito and Romola. Like Tito, the Friar is a flawed character, and at the end of chapter 25 the narrator emphasises that this famous historical personage will be presented warts and all. These blemishes, however, are pointed up in a way very different from that used to present Tito's. Savonarola is presented mainly through outside views. One sees his effect on Romola; one is given the community point of view concerning him; and occasionally historical generalisations are offered. The text of one of his sermons is transcribed and the effect on its auditors noted; and his political machinations are analysed by Machiavelli himself. But very little use is made of psychological omniscience and when it is employed the reader is summarily told something rather than shown.

As a result, while the reader is always kept very close to Tito and

Romola and is usually inside their heads, one always has the sense
of being at a certain distance from the Friar and having only a dim
comprehension of the sources of his visionary power and of that
'subtle mysterious influence of a personality by which it has been
given to some rare men to move their fellows' (ch. 15). G.H. Lewes
was never more annoyingly glib than when he told Blackwood that
Marian 'knows infinitely more about Savonarola than she knew of
Silas' (*L*, iii, 420). On the contrary, the narrator of *Silas Marner*
knew everything about the title character and psychological omniscience was magisterially employed in giving the reader an
intimate felt sense of the inner processes by which the weaver is
recalled to life. In contrast, it would seem that the visionary power
at the core of Savonarola's inner life cannot be illuminated by the
tools of psychological omniscience. Moral and psychological
depths can be probed, but not (at least in *Romola*) spiritual ones.

The absence of substantiation, however, should not keep one
from noting an important new departure in *Romola*: an interest in
visionary experience – in 'the shadowy region where human souls
seek wisdom apart from the human sympathies which are the very
life and substance of our wisdom' (ch. 15). One of the advantages
afforded by the historical setting was the various examples it
offered of visionary types, including Romola's brother Dino, who
believes that his dying vision is a revelation meant for his sister;
and, of course, Savonarola himself, who believes that God has
made his purpose present to him through visions. Questions
concerning the genuineness and provenance of visionary experience are raised in the text of *Romola*. Visions are no exception to the
epistemological rule cited by a number of characters: meaning (of a
painting or a face, for example) and interpretation (as of a character
or a text) are dependent on point of view. As a minor character
observes: 'there is as wonderful a power of stretching in the
meaning of visions as in Dido's bull's hide. It seems to me a dream
may mean whatever comes after it' (ch. 29). There is an analogous
recognition that visions may be influenced if not determined by the
predisposition of the visionary. And it is important to note that
none of the visions mentioned or described in *Romola* is authenti-
cated by the narrator. On the other hand, there are no narratorial
dismissals of visionary experience either, though there is a strong
predisposition (how could there not be in a novel by Marian Evans)
in favour of human sympathies rather than a wisdom set apart
from them.

Ultimately the novel's position on visionary experience is the same as that of its central character. Romola sounds dismissive when she exclaims to her brother: 'What is this religion of yours, that places visions before natural duties?' and a later question of hers is equally rhetorical: 'What had the words of that vision to do with her real sorrows?' (chs. 15, 36). But when Tito suggests that her brother's vision 'was an ordinary monkish vision, bred of fasting and fanatical ideas', Romola's answer is equivocal; 'poor Dino, *he* believed it was a divine message. It is strange, this life of men possessed with fervid beliefs that seem like madness to their fellow-beings. Dino was not a vulgar fanatic'. And as for Savonarola: 'his very voice seemed to have penetrated me with a sense that there is some truth in what moves [visionaries]: some truth of which I know nothing' (ch. 17). Tito later tells his wife 'to take care . . . you have a touch of fanaticism in you. I shall have you seeing visions, like your brother' (ch. 27). This does not happen, though in a way one wishes it had: like Maggie Tulliver's drifting away at the end of *The Mill on the Floss*, chapters 61 and 68 of *Romola* would be less troublesome if their romantic and symbolic elements could be assigned to the visionary capabilities of the central character rather than to the author. Nonetheless, in *Romola*, for the first but not the last time in a George Eliot novel, visionary experience is an important concern.

As Marian remarked, she began *Romola* a young woman and finished it an old one. During the 1860s she was often ill and/or depressed. Throughout her writing career Marian complained of the demands of creative composition; but the following journal entry from February 1862, when she was struggling to get *Romola* off the ground, is exceptional: 'I have been very ailing all this last week and have worked under impending discouragement. I have a distrust in myself, in my work, in others' loving acceptance of it which robs my otherwise happy life of all joy. I ask myself, without being able to answer, whether I have ever before felt so chilled and oppressed' (*L*, iv, 17). And two and a half years later there is an even more striking entry: 'Horrible scepticism about all things paralysing my mind. Shall I ever be good for anything again? Ever do anything again?' (Cross, II, 299–300).

Marian's physical and psychological exacerbations during this period are the subject of Miriam Allott's suggestive essay, 'George Eliot in the 1860s'. She argues that there is a close connection between them and Marian's 'ebbing creative vitality' during the decade, a dulling of the creative sensibility that led to the substitution of 'didactic earnestness and painstaking research combined with emotional exhortation', all of which encouraged her 'worst faults – her tendency to sermonize, her fits of self-righteousness, her wooden contrivances'. Allott calls attention to Marian's increasing interest during the decade not simply in determination by deeds but in determination by foregoing hereditary conditions; and she makes the telling point that the only experience during this period that Marian is 'able to realise with genuine imaginative success is that of personal despair' (the reference is to Mrs Transome's sins coming home to roost in *Felix Holt*).[4]

The principal disappointment in Allott's paper is her lack of interest in diagnosing the cause of her subject's creative malaise. *Prima facie*, there is a good deal to suggest that during this period Marian experienced a mid-life crisis of the kind that formed a watershed in the careers of a number of nineteenth-century writers. The precipitates and/or symptoms of this crisis are a sharpened awareness of mortality and the sense that, perceptually and creatively, something has fled – a loss that makes earlier works seem fantastications and fresh creative achievement impossible. 'A power is gone, which nothing can restore', says Wordsworth in his 'Elegiac Stanzas'; 'a deep distress' (his brother's death) has made earlier beliefs and powers seem fond illusions. And Whitman, in his great 1860 poem, 'As I Ebb'd with the Ocean of Life', can see no principle of continuity between his present self – 'baffled, balk'd, bent to the very earth, / Oppress'd with myself that I have dared to open my mouth' – and that 'electric self' out of the pride of which he had earlier offered confident proclamations.

On the other side of the watershed for both Wordsworth and Whitman was what the former called the philosophic mind. The later works of Marian Evans are similarly marked by the increased importance played in them by ideas. Henry James observed that at the outset of her creative life 'perception and reflection' divided the 'great talent' of Marian Evans between them; but that 'as time went on circumstances led the latter to develop at the expense of the former' and that it was in *Romola* that the equilibrium was lost. James does not seem to have considered a psychological explanation. He thought the influence of Lewes a sufficient reason, especially given his growing interest in science and cosmic problems. This, thought James, was the chief circumstance that had tipped the balance further than it would otherwise have gone in the direction of reflection and of systematic scientific observation as distinguished from the copious natural observation found in the early novels (*CH*, 498–9).

The system that had the most important influence on Marian's reflective predisposition was the Positivism of Auguste Comte. Lewes had long been an important English expositor and promulgator of the views of the French thinker, and Marian had become more exposed to these ideas after 1859 when a close friendship developed between her and Richard and Maria Congreve, the former of whom was Comte's principal English adherent. The aspect of Positivism perhaps most pertinent to Marian's intellectual background was the way in which it carried forward the materialist critique of Feuerbach. As Engels explained, the doctrine of Feuerbach amounted to materialism in all but name. The author of *The Essence of Christianity*, however, had been reluctant to use the name because he had confused 'the materialism that is a general world outlook resting upon a definite conception of the relation between matter and mind' with the static, mechanical form in which this outlook had been expressed during the eighteenth century. In the nineteenth century the rise of the natural sciences and the life sciences had discredited this unhistorical view of the world of nature and replaced it with a model of the universe 'as a process – as matter developing in an historical process'. This conception remained unavailable to Feuerbach, as did the human analogy: that 'we live not only in nature but also in human society, and this also no less than nature has its history of development and its science . . . the science of society (i.e., the sum total of the so-called historical and philosophical sciences)'.[5]

The essence of Comte's Positivism was the belief in the Religion of Humanity. As a result of historical progress and centuries of scientific and philosophical advances, this religion had at last come to supersede Christianity. Before this stage was reached society had to pass through two antecedent stages: the theological and the metaphysical. In the first, the explanation of phenomena and of events was thought to be found in the operations of supernatural beings. In the second, abstractions or what Bentham called fictitious entities were thought to explain phenomena. In the final stage, the Positivist, it was recognised that there was nothing higher than mankind, and that there could be no knowledge that was not experientially derived. In their development the sciences passed through similar phases and in the nineteenth century the highest of the sciences, the social science, had begun to yield verifiable information about man and society.

In Comte's *oeuvre*, analysis of the past progress of society was followed by speculation concerning society's ethical and religious future. As John Stuart Mill explained, Comte referred 'the obligations of duty, as well as all sentiments of devotion, to a concrete object, at once ideal and real; the Human Race, conceived as a continuous whole, including the past, the present, and the future'. Many others had perceived the power that 'the idea of the general interest of the human race, both as a source of emotion and as a motive to conduct', could come to have over the mind; but no one had realised as fully 'all the majesty of which that idea is susceptible'. For Comte the good of the human race became 'the ultimate standard of right and wrong'. The cardinal tenet of morality was to live for others. The object of all education and moral discipline was 'to make altruism (a word of his own coining) predominate over egoism'.[6] The bedrock human instincts, like the sexual instinct and that of self-preservation, were egotistic. But there were also altruistic propensities in man which led to love and respect for individuals, and could lead, if the egotistic propensities became sufficiently recessive, to the love of communities and then to the highest feeling known to man, love of humanity. Just as the sexual instinct was the most disturbing of the egotistic propensities, so the conjugal love found in marriage was the most important means of converting egotism into its opposite. Not for nothing did women, who represented the affective, loving element in human nature, occupy a central position in the religious observances of Positivist worship, the central figure of which was the Madonna.

It is not hard to find evidence of the influence of Comte's thought in Marian's later work. If one is so inclined, the whole of *Romola* can be read as a Positivist allegory; and there is no other way to read the novel's patently symbolical chapters 61 and 68. In the former Romola is gripped by despair. She has lost her faith in Savonarola and knows no answers to the question: 'What force was there to create for her that supremely hallowed motive which men call duty, but which can have no inward constraining existence save through some form of believing love?' She has lost the vision of 'any great purpose, any end of existence which could ennoble endurance and exalt the common deeds of dusty life with divine ardours'. She feels herself sinking into 'barren egoistic complaining' that life could bring her no content. Longing for the repose of mere sensation, Romola procures a boat, glides away on the deepening waters, and sleeps. When she awakes seven chapters later, she finds that instead of bringing her to death, the boat has been 'the gently lulling cradle of a new life'. The cry of a child first draws her attention to a plague-stricken village where she devotes herself to caring for the sick. She is believed by the villagers to be 'the Holy Mother, come to take care of the people'. And after she leaves, 'many legends were . . . told in that valley about the blessed Lady who came over the sea'. Her experience in the village is like a new baptism to Romola; she finds in the primary altruistic relations of a human being to his fellow-man the form of sustaining love that can provide life with a sense of purpose and even with an eschatological dimension. She has, that is, evolved from a belief in Christianity to a belief in the Religion of Humanity.

The Comtean allegory in these chapters is patent, but only here and in one other place – the poem 'O may I join the choir invisible' – is it possible to find anything so overtly doctrinal. While Marian considered Comte a great thinker and acknowledged a debt to him, she was no more a committed Positivist than she was a committed feminist. The most important influence of Positivist thinking on her creative work is not found in any specific doctrines but in the impetus it gave to a change in her aesthetic thinking. In 1866 Frederic Harrison, a social reformer and follower of Comte, wrote to Marian urging her to devote her creative energies to the promulgation of Positivist ideas. In her reply, Marian cautioned Harrison that he had laid a 'tremendously difficult problem' before her. She spoke as one who had 'gone through again and again the severe effort of trying to make certain ideas thoroughly incarnate, as if they had revealed themselves to me first in the flesh and not in the spirit'. She considered what she called 'aesthetic teaching' to be 'the highest of all teaching because it deals with life in its highest complexity'. But 'if it ceases to be purely aesthetic teaching – if it lapses anywhere from the picture to the diagram – it becomes the most offensive of all teaching' (*L*, iv, 300). And in a letter written twelve years later she named another key caveat of her post-*Romola* conception of herself as artist: 'My function is that of the *aesthetic*, not the doctrinal teacher – the rousing of the nobler emotions, which make mankind desire the social right, not the prescribing of special measures, concerning which the artistic mind, however strongly moved by social sympathy, is often not the best judge' (*L*, vii, 44).

To a point, this line of aesthetic thinking can be thought an extension of the views on art and the artist that Marian expressed in her essays of the mid-1850s and embodied in her early novels. Ideas tend to replace memories as the germs or millet seeds of her creative works; but the importance of the picture – the representation, the showing – is reaffirmed. So, too, the principle that the task of the literary artist is not to disseminate ideas, and certainly not to specify courses of action, but to act on the emotions of readers. And there would seem to be a difference only in degree and not in kind between 'the extension of our sympathies' as described in 'The Natural History of German Life' (1856) and 'the rousing of the nobler emotions' mentioned in her 1878 letter. Both the sympathy that is 'the raw material of moral sentiment' and the nobler emotions are altruistic (though at different ends of the other-regarding scale) and as such both are inimical to all the varieties of egotism.

What is different are the means employed to stimulate the emotions. In 1855 Marian had specified 'the sense in which every great artist is a teacher – namely, by giving us his higher sensibility as a medium . . . bringing home to our coarser senses what would otherwise be unperceived by us' (*Essays*, 126). But in the later novels it is often less a matter of perceptions than of convictions incarnated in sometimes idealised forms. Furthermore, it is necessary to take at a considerable discount Marian's insistence in a letter of 1876, apropos of a distinction her correspondent had seemed to make between 'my earlier and later works', that there had been 'no change in the point of view from which I regard our life since I wrote my first fiction' (*L*, vi, 318). The perspective may be the same, but the predisposition of the perceiver and the focusing instrument are not.

Another key difference between Marian's earlier and later aesthetic thinking is the influence on the latter of her scientific interests. One example is the increased emphasis on the formal and organic qualities of a work of art. Her ideal as an artist, she told a correspondent in 1873, was 'to make matter and form an inseparable truthfulness' (*L*, v, 374). And the 1868 'Notes on Form in Art' is a highly condensed and elliptical series of reflections on 'what relations of things can be properly included under the word Form as applied to artistic composition' (*Essays*, 432). It is impossible to imagine Marian having written these notes in the 1850s or early 1860s; nor would she then have used the scientific metaphor she did in 1876 in describing her writing as 'simply a set of experiments in life' (*L*, vi, 216). In the later novels the appropriate image of the author is no longer a seventeenth-century Dutch painter or an Egyptian sorcerer but rather a scientist like Lydgate in *Middlemarch*, whose professional ambitions, as described in an extraordinary passage in chapter 16, are at the same time a description of the methods and ambitions of the novel's narrator. Or, to cite another of Marian's self-images, the author of the later novels resembles the description of Dante in the essay about false testimonials in her last book, *Impressions of Theophrastus Such*. There the author of *The Divine Comedy* is made to sound as much like an experimental scientist as a visionary. Dante's 'powerful imagination is not false outward vision, but intense inward representation, and a creative energy constantly fed by susceptibility to the veriest minutiae of experience'. There is no 'confusion of provable fact with the fictions of fancy and transient inclination'; but rather 'a breadth of ideal association which informs every material object, every incidental fact . . . bringing into new light the less obvious relations of human existence'.[7]

It was principally in the last two novels, *Middlemarch* and *Daniel Deronda*, that such intense representations are found. In the late 1860s Marian devoted much of her energies to the medium of poetry, which was free from the representational constraints of realistic prose fiction. It is obvious that her interest in writing poetry is directly related to the increased importance that ideas had come to have in her aesthetic thinking. When she sent Blackwood the manuscript of *The Legend of Jubal and Other Poems* (1874), she told him that every one of the eleven pieces (to which four were added in later editions) 'represents an idea which I care for strongly and wish to propagate as far as I can. Else I should forbid myself from adding to the mountainous heap of poetical collections' (*L*, vi, 26). In reading this volume and *The Spanish Gypsy* (1868), the book-length poem which she struggled to keep under 9000 lines, one is reminded more than once or twice of Mallarmé's reply to Degas' complaint that he had been unsuccessful in his attempts to write sonnets despite all the ideas that he had: 'You don't write poems with ideas, my dear Degas, but with words'. Marian said of the poems of Matthew Arnold that while she could have given them only tepid praise after reading them once, 'after reading them again and again, we have become their partizan, and are tempted to become intolerant of those who will not admit their beauty' (*WR*, 64 [1855], 297). After reading and rereading the poetry of Marian Evans, one wishes one could be as positive; alas, I should be more tempted to say of her verse what Edith Sitwell said of Arnold's: that those who like it dislike poetry. But Marian certainly took the writing of poetry seriously and even spoke of it as 'a new organ, a new medium that my nature had languished for' (*L*, iv, 465), and one would like to respect her seriousness by taking the poems seriously. Fortunately, there are two non-verbal points of view from which some of her poems are of real interest: their working out and/or vigorous presentation of passionately-held ideas; and Marian's thoughtful attempts to adapt different poetic forms and genres to her communicative urges.

'Armgart', examined in the previous chapter, is an example of a poem containing both points of interest. So is the 850-line 'A College Breakfast-Party', which Marian described as 'A Symposium . . . a poetic dialogue embodying . . . the actual contest of ideas' (*L*, vi, 388). The fine mind of the author is much in evidence in this lively recreation of high-flying undergraduate disputation. The supple flow of the poem's blank verse and its pro-contra crispness recall Browning's 'Bishop Blougram's Apology', about which Marian had been particularly enthusiastic in her review of *Men and Women* and to which her own debate poem is clearly indebted.

'The Legend of Jubal', the title poem of the 1874 collection, is a more ambitious performance. It is a mythical narrative of Marian's own concoction, consisting of more than 900 lines of iambic pentameter couplets, the fluid movement of which derives from Leigh Hunt and the Keats of *Endymion*, with a bracing additive from Swinburne's 1866 poem 'Anactoria'. The speaker of Swinburne's poem is Sappho, the founder of lyric poetry in the Greek tradition. The title character of Marian's poem is put forward as the founder of poetry in the Hebraic tradition. The offspring of Cain have lived happily in the land east of Eden until the shadow of death falls on them. In some, the felt knowledge of mortality becomes the spur of high ambition and heroic action. For such, as for Tennyson's Ulysses, some work of noble note may yet be done before death closes all. Of the three sons of Lamech, one turns to the animal world, tames the beasts and becomes the founder of pastoral life; the second exploits the power of fire and becomes the prototype of

technological man. The third son is Jubal, who in a visionary
moment sees that his destiny is creative, fashions a lyre, practices
singing to its accompaniment, and when he is ready comes down
from the hills to share with his people his hitherto solitary joy:

> It was at evening,
> When shadows lengthen from each westward thing,
> When imminence of change makes sense more fine
> And light seems holier in its grand decline.

Jubal's song satisfies some 'strange thirst', some unnamed discon-
tent, in his listeners. Visionary urges then take him away from his
people. He returns as an old man to find that while no one
remembers him as a person, his name is on everyone's lips because
of the great gift he had brought them. In his dying vision, Jubal
realises exactly what Sappho does at the climax of Swinburne's poem:
that the recompense for his mortality is the immortality of song.

It is in two of her shorter compositions that Marian was most
poetically successful: 'Brother and Sister' and 'O may I join the
choir invisible'. She described the former as 'little descriptive bits
on the mutual influences' in the childhood lives of a brother and
sister (*L*, v, 403). The form that she chose to contain these bits of
affectionate recollection was that of the Shakespearean sonnet with
its three quatrains and closing couplet. It was a good choice; each
of the eleven sonnets is a discrete entity that can accommodate
particularised descriptions as well as then/now generalisations.
The closing couplet is particularly well utilised. Sometimes it nicely
rounds off the preceding stanzas; at other times it is used to
introduce an adult perspective as a gloss on the childhood experience. An example is found in the finest sonnet, which describes a
mildly sublime expansion of consciousness experience in which
the outside world becomes fused with the growing self of the
perceiver:

> Our brown canal was endless to my thought;
> And on its banks I sat in dreamy peace,
> Unknowing how the good I loved was wrought,
> Untroubled by the fear that it would cease.
>
> Slowly the barges floated into view,
> Rounding a grassy hill to me sublime

With some Unknown behind it, whither flew
The parting cuckoo toward a fresh spring-time.

The wide-arched bridge, the scented elder-flowers,
The wondrous watery rings that died too soon,
The echoes of the quarry, the still hours
With white robe sweeping on the shadeless noon,

Were but my growing self, are part of me,
My present Past, my root of piety.

At the same time each sonnet is linked to the others by a narrative line (the siblings leaving home to go fishing together, traversing well-known spots, and reaching the brown canal where the sister catches a fish) as well as by a certain retrospective impetus that begins by forcing the speaker back into the past ('I cannot choose but think upon the time . . .') and ends abruptly by speaking of the inevitable severance of the sibling bond first by school and then by 'the dire years whose awful name is Change'.

In 'O may I join the choir invisible' the form of a Christian hymn and Christian imagery are boldly utilised to provide the vehicle for a wholly Positivist tenor. This appropriation enables the poet to foreground the eschatological dimension of the Religion of Humanity which could only be vaguely figured forth in *Romola*. The invisible choir is not the cherubim and seraphim, not the communion of saints, but 'those immortal dead who live again / In minds made better by their presence'.

The *imitatio Christi* becomes the imperative of striving to emulate the deeds of those who have gone before. The Eucharist becomes not the visual representation of Christ's body but a 'worthier image for the sanctuary': the ideal image of a 'divinely human' self; the Christian mystical body is transformed into the evolving body of humanity – 'the growing life of man'; and the Christian life to come becomes the living again in the pulses and thoughts of those inspired by our example. And at the end of the poem there is a masterly appropriation of the figure of paradox used in the celebration of the Christian mysteries when the poet speaks of 'the sweet presence of a good diffused' that is 'in diffusion ever more intense' – an intense diffusion of Positivist ideas being exactly what the poem accomplishes.

This leaves us with *The Spanish Gypsy*, Marian's longest and most

sustained attempt at poetic composition. Its subject was suggested
to her by a picture of the Annunciation seen at Venice in May 1864,
which prompted a train of reflection leading to the thought that
'here was a great dramatic motive', never before used, that was 'of
the same class as those used by the Greek dramatists, yet specifi-
cally differing from them':

> A young maiden, believing herself to be on the eve of the chief
> event of her life – marriage – about to share in the ordinary lot of
> womanhood, full of young hope, has suddenly announced to
> her that she is chosen to fulfil a great destiny, entailing a terribly
> different experience from that of ordinary womanhood. She is
> chosen, not by any momentary arbitrariness, but as a result of
> foregoing hereditary conditions: she obeys. 'Behold the hand-
> maid of the Lord.'

The next step was to give 'the motive a clothing in some suitable
set of historical and local conditions' (Cross, iii, 32). This was
found in the moment in Spanish history in the late fifteenth
century when the struggle against the Moors was reaching its
climax and there were gypsies present under conditions suitable
for having an hereditary claim laid on a young woman.

Work on the verse drama went on slowly and painfully, partially
because Marian had no pre-existent story to work from and had to
'work out the dramatic action for [herself] under the inspiration of
[her] idea' (*L*, iv, 301). There was, however, at least one antecedent
work that provided some guidance. In both her verse drama and in
Romola the necessary idealisation is attained by adopting the clothing
of the past: both works are set in southern Europe in the late 1400s
at times of historical ferment. Both open with the same thick
impasto of local detail and a similar buzz of gossip. Both have a
similarly idealised title character whose experience of the joy of
first love is eventually superseded by sorrow, renunciation and a
life of service to others. And the crucial recognition scene in the
poem, when Fedalma's eyes meet those of her captive father while
he is being led across the Plaça Santiago, all too obviously copies
the recognition scene in chapter 22 of *Romola* between Tito and his
father in the Piazzi del Duomo.

A final point of resemblance is that both works show an 'extraordinary rhetorical energy'. This was the first point about *The
Spanish Gypsy* made by Henry James in his review, in which he was

clearly at pains to do all that he in conscience could to accentuate the positive. James was nonetheless forced to observe that the poem was wanting in passion and gave off a perpetual sense of effort, that its dramatic aspects were deficient, that an 'indefinably factitious air' surrounded its characters, 'which is not sufficiently justified by their position as ideal figures', and that the background of the action was 'cold and mechanical as a whole'.[8] He might have added that the work was not so much romantic and symbolical, as Marian had described chapters 61 and 68 of *Romola*, as operatic and declamatory.

But there is the rhetorical energy as well as the intellectual vigour with which the central thematic issues are worked out. The concern with foregoing hereditary conditions is not confined to the three central characters, Fedalma, her father Zarca and Duke Silva. It is found in the repellent opinions of the Prior, who believes that internal characteristics are genetically transmitted; in the Jew Sephardo who believes in the overarching importance of racial identity; in the book of King Alfonso, which states that of the ways in which a man acquires nobility, lineage is the first and most important and valour and worthy behaviour third and last; and in the musical skill of Pablo which (like Fedalma's talent as a dancer) seems half inherited and half acquired.

Zarca, the gypsy chieftain, is distinguished by his heroic singleness of purpose. He holds at the tribal level a version of the Positivist faith expressed in 'O may I join the choir invisible': he himself must be a great hero in order to give the Gypsy race great memories that will inspire them and lead them outward and upward. He intends to take his people to a promised land beyond the sea, and in a striking speech that mixes Faustian striving with Positivist meliorism he encourages Fedalma to strengthen her resolve to become his heir. But acceptance of her racial destiny entails the extinction of her young joy. She must take 'This yearning self of mine and strangle it'. Her resolve is waning in the second half of the poem when Silva, formerly her betrothed, visits her in the Gypsy camp and urges her to reunite her life with his. Though the terminology is different, their ensuing debate is essentially a reprise of that between Stephen Guest and Maggie Tulliver in the closing section of *The Mill on the Floss*. There is one key difference, however, which epitomises the shift in emphasis between the earlier and later works of George Eliot. Silva and Stephen both represent the claims of the present; but while Maggie upholds the claims of the personal *past*, the hereditary ties that bind Fedalma relate to the *future* of her race.

As one reaches the closing scenes of *The Spanish Gypsy*, it is not at all clear how the conflicts explored in the body of the work will be resolved, though no reader familiar with the previous work of Marian Evans will expect the granting of Silva's wish for a supernatural resolution of his and Fedalma's plight (in which fond hope the Duke resembles no one so much as a reluctantly doubting Victorian searching for a reassuring sign from above). Marian herself had difficulty in deciding on the poem's ending and eventually returned to her original conception, which is distinctly problematic. Zarca captures Bedmár from the Spanish; a late scene shows him sleeping soundly near three corpses he has mercilessly slain; and Father Isodor is brutally hanged. This barbaric *réal politique* causes Silva first to renounce the Gypsy identity he had embraced in order to reunite himself with Fedalma, and then to murder Zarca. It is therefore his daughter who will lead her people to the promised land over the sea. But Fedalma already foresees what in historical fact was to be the case: the non-realisation of Zarca's visionary hopes for his race. In the final tableau Fedalma and Silva part forever. The closing lines of *The Spanish Gypsy*, describing the 'long gaze of their renouncing love', are not unimpressive and even bring to mind such well-known Victorian poetic closures as those to Arnold's *Sohrab and Rustum* and Tennyson's *Idylls of the King*:

> It was night
> Before the ships weighed anchor and gave sail;
> Fresh night emergent in her clearness, lit
> By the large crescent moon, with Hesperus
> And those great stars that lead the eager host.
> Fedalma stood and watched the little bark
> Lying jet-black upon moon-whitened waves.
> Silva was standing too. He too divined
> A steadfast form that held him with its thought
> And eyes that sought him vanishing: he saw
> The waters widen slowly, till at last
> Straining he gazed and knew not if he gazed
> On aught but blackness overhung by stars.

7

Felix Holt (1866) and *Middlemarch* (1871–72)

'What do I think of *Middlemarch*?' What do I think of glory . . .
The mysteries of human nature surpass the 'mysteries of redemp-
tion.'

Emily Dickinson

In 1848 revolutionary events on the continent had prompted Marian
Evans to make one of her infrequent comments on the social and
political situation in her own country:

> Our working classes are eminently inferior to the mass of the
> French people. In France, the *mind* of the people is highly
> electrified – they are full of ideas on social subjects – they really
> desire social *reform* – not merely an acting out of Sancho Panza's
> favourite proverb 'Yesterday for you, to-day for me.' The revol-
> utionary animus extended over the whole nation, and embraced
> the rural population – not merely as with us, the artisans of the
> towns. Here there is so much larger a proportion of selfish
> radicalism and unsatisfied, brute sensuality (in the agricultural
> and mining districts especially) than of perception or desire of
> justice, that a revolutionary movement would be simply destruc-
> tive – not constructive. Besides, it would be put down. Our
> military have no notion of 'fraternizing.' They have the same
> sort of inveteracy as dogs have for the ill-drest canaille. They are
> as mere a brute force as a battering ram and the aristocracy have
> got firm hold of them. Our little humbug of a queen is more
> endurable than the rest of her race because she calls forth a
> chivalrous feeling, and there is nothing in our constitution to
> obstruct the slow progress of *political* reform. This is all we are fit
> for at present. The social reform which may prepare us for great
> changes is more and more the object of effort both in Parliament

and out of it. But we English are slow crawlers.

(*L*, i, 254)

The essential conservatism and gradualist bias of Marian's mind is as evident in this passage as in other texts previously examined: the October 1843 letter to Sara Hennell concerning the truth of feeling, in which 'the only safe revolution' for both individuals and nations is said to be that which arises out of the wants their own progress has generated; the 1852 article on Margaret Fuller and Mary Wollstonecraft, in which 'little by little' is identified as 'the only way in which human things can be mended'; 'The Natural History of German Life' (1856), in which Riehl's social–political conservatism is endorsed; and the 1867 letter to John Morley, in which a gradual moral evolution is seen as the only means through which 'an approach to equivalence of good for men and women' can succeed.

Against this background an extraordinary passage in chapter 32 of *The Mill on the Floss* stands out strongly. The narrator is speaking of the 'tone of emphasis' one falls into in referring to 'the history of unfashionable families' and of how far it is from the tone of 'good society':

But then, good society has its claret and its velvet-carpets, its dinner-engagements six weeks deep, its opera and its faëry ball-rooms; rides off its ennui on thoroughbred horses, lounges at the club, has to keep clear of crinoline vortices, gets its science done by Faraday, and its religion by the superior clergy who are to be met in the best houses: how should it have time or need for belief and emphasis? But good society, floated on gossamer wings of light irony, is of very expensive production; requiring nothing less than a wide and arduous national life condensed in unfragrant deafening factories, cramping itself in mines, sweating at furnaces, grinding, hammering, weaving under more or less oppression of carbonic acid – or else, spread over sheepwalks, and scattered in lonely houses and huts on the clayey or chalky corn-lands, where the rainy days look dreary. This wide national life is based entirely on emphasis – the emphasis of want, which urges it into all the activities necessary for the maintenance of good society and light irony: it spends its heavy years often in a chill uncarpeted fashion, amidst family discord unsoftened by long corridors.

The quality of moral outrage in this passage concerning the two nations into which Britain is divided, and the insistence on the interconnectedness of the two, recalls the radical social vision of Carlyle in *Past and Present*, of Ruskin in 'The Nature of Gothic' chapter of *The Stones of Venice*, and of Dickens in his great social anatomies of the 1850s, *Bleak House* and *Little Dorritt*. What it does not sound like is Marian Evans. The passage is unique in her canon, and for all its impressiveness must ultimately be regarded simply as another example of the expressive distortions found in her second novel.

It is not until *Felix Holt, The Radical*, begun in March 1865, that one finds Marian deeply engaged with the condition of England question. The engagement is owing to the changed social and political climate of the mid-1860s, by which time two decades of relative economic prosperity and the relative absence of divisive political issues had given way to increasing social and political tensions. A chief cause was the agitation stemming from demands that the working classes be given the vote. In 1864 Gladstone had declared himself in favour of an extension of the franchise, which was finally secured by the passage of the second Reform Bill in 1867. But in mid-decade these and other issues had revived fears – largely dormant since the 1840s – of possibly violent social upheavals.

Marian's way of responding creatively to current events was entirely typical of her. In her next two novels she went back in time – to 'Loamshire' in the early 1830s during the time of unrest leading to the passage of the first Reform Bill in 1832, which had enfranchised the middle classes. She did not return to the turn-of-the-century world of *Adam Bede* and *Silas Marner* that had provided models of *community*, but to the *society* of two midland towns and their environs: Nuneaton, the Treby Magna of *Felix Holt*, and Coventry, which is called Middlemarch. Both towns are seen under the aspect of change. Each 'history', as the novels are called by their narrators, 'is chiefly concerned with the private lot of a few men and women; but there is no private life which has not been determined by a wider public life' (*Felix Holt*, ch. 3). It is through a detailed recreation and study of this interaction in the preceding generation that Marian hoped to contribute to an understanding of the social and political situation of the late 1860s. As she would remark in a late note on the 'historic imagination': the 'exercise of a veracious imagination in historical picturing' was 'capable of a development that might help the judgment greatly with regard to present and future events . . . I mean the working out in detail of the various steps by which a political or social change was reached . . . For want of such real, minute vision of how changes come about in the past, we fall into ridiculously inconsistent estimates of actual movements' (*Essays*, 446–7).

Up to a point *Felix Holt* can be described as a political novel. The historical moment during which it is set is a time 'when faith in the efficacy of political change was at fever-heat in ardent Reformers' (ch. 16). Events in the novel take place within the time frame of an election and are related to its phases – the nomination meetings, speeches and machinations of election agents that precede the novel's big set piece: the account of Election Day in Treby Magna. *Felix Holt* is also political in that Marian has taken the opportunity to vent her own political views through her title character, a mouthpiece she found it convenient to use again in her 1868 article, 'Address to Working Men, by Felix Holt'. These views are opposed to others represented in the novel: the unreflective Tory position put by Mr Wace, the brewer: 'there's a right in things. The heavy end will get downmost. And if Church and King, and every man being sure of his own, are things good for this country, there's a God above will take care of 'em' (ch. 20); the rational radicalism of Harold Transome, who thinks that the dead wood in society must be removed and replaced and that 'the inevitable process of changing everything' ought to be accomplished by enlightened persons like himself and not by 'beggarly demagogues and purse-proud tradesmen' (ch. 2); and the resentment-laden radicalism of the trades union man, who views politics as a class struggle between the few and the many. Felix's views are distinctly different from each of these. He is not a democrat insisting on universal (male) suffrage and he is more concerned with individual moral change than with change in institutions. He believes that the working classes should be helped to become sober, responsible, better-educated and able to help themselves. For him, changes are only good in proportion as 'they put knowledge in place of ignorance, and fellow-feeling in the place of selfishness' (*Essays*, 422). Everything that Felix is most against is epitomised by the Election Day mob, 'in which the multitudinous small wickednesses of small selfish ends . . . undirected towards any larger result, had issued in widely-shared mischief that might yet be hideous' (ch. 33).

But, as one would expect from a work in which the positives are firmly located in individual moral conduct, *Felix Holt* is a political novel only in a limited sense. The qualities and destinies of the characters are not seen in political terms, but in moral and spiritual terms; and the crucial positive determinants are fellow-feeling and the capacity for vision. As the narrator of *Middlemarch* will say: 'Our good depends on the quality and breadth of our emotion' (ch. 47). At the beginning of *Felix Holt*, a social and political contrast is established between the two central male characters, both of whom are radicals: Harold Transome, a gentleman and heir to his family's estate, and Felix Holt, a common man, son of a purveyor of quack medicines and a dissenting mother who lives up a back street. But the contrast between them is brought into focus by Esther Lyon and the marriage plot. Whom Esther will marry is the dominant question in the novel's second half, and the scrutiny to which the two men in her life are subjected is moral and emotional. The key point about Harold Transome is not the quality of his political ideas, but the quality of his attitude to others, especially to women. Esther comes to realise that there is 'an air of moral mediocrity' about him, an egotism that 'had a way of virtually measuring the value of everything by the contribution it made to his own plea-sure'. For this reason even his good nature comes to be unsym-pathetic to her because 'it never came from any thorough understanding or deep respect for what was in the mind of the person he obliged or indulged' (ch. 43).

In marrying Felix, Esther does indeed make a class choice: the reason for the cumbersome legal plot is precisely to put her in the position of being able to renounce the Transome estate for an obscure life of good works with a man of the people. But the centre of interest in Esther's development – from the young woman with superior airs who reads *René* and Byron's poetry and cannot abide the smell of tallow candles, through 'the first self-questioning, the first voluntary subjection, the first longing to acquire the strength of greater motives' (ch. 27), to her final victory over worldly wisdom – is in the education of her feelings and her moral and spiritual growth.

No wonder, then, that a commentator like Arnold Kettle found *Felix Holt* disappointing. He much admired its first hundred pages, in which radicalism was seen 'not simply as a set of opinions' but as 'a social force arising out of basic economic changes' and in which personal stories seemed 'essentially determined' by the wider public life of Treby and 'organically bound up with the condition of England, with class-conflicts and the moral problems involved in social advance'. But for Kettle the novel failed to fulfil its promise. This was owing to the author's failure 'to face, morally or artistically, the problems she has set in motion'. When it came to 'the question of change, of tackling the real problems implicit and explicit in the democratization of British society', what stood out in Marian's attitude (as in Matthew Arnold's contemporaneous *Culture and Anarchy*) was the middle-class intellectual's fear of the mob.[1]

From another point of view, however, the principal failing in *Felix Holt* can be said to lie elsewhere: in the imperfect articulation of its moral and spiritual concerns. For Peter Coveney the novel's 'great flaw' is that the political framework of an election does not allow for the adequate development of its 'moral content'.[2] This criticism is equally *à point*. There is something too schematic and too notional about the stages in Esther's development; and the principal force for good in her life, the title character, is a wholly idealised figure. The other centre of moral interest in the novel, Harold's mother Mrs Transome, is much more effectively realised. For one thing, her story is brought into sharper focus through its contrast with that of Mr Lyon, the dissenting minister, who also has a hidden secret in his past concerning the parentage of his child. But Rufus Lyon is defined not by his past but by his capacity for vision, which gives him a wider sense 'of past and present realities' and brings him into contact with 'the larger sweep of the world's forces' (ch. 16). It is Felix who says that 'we are saved by making the future present to ourselves' (ch. 27), but it is Mr Lyon who is the embodiment of this truth.

Mr Lyon's visionary propensities are rooted in his dissenting chapel background, which is the antithesis of Mrs Transome's conservative Anglicanism, just as his contact with larger forces outside the self is the opposite of the inexorable tightening grip of the past upon her, and of her intense self-concern, which has reduced 'the great story of this world . . . to the little tale of her own existence' (ch. 34). Mrs Transome's only future concern is that her secret sin will be revealed: the illegitimacy of her son, the product of an adulterous affair years before with the lawyer Jermyn. A man who epitomises 'the ambitions of pushing middle-class gentility', Jermyn radiates a 'moral vulgarity [which] cleaved to him like an hereditary odour', and his consciousness at the age of sixty shows the effects of 'a selfishness which has spread its fibres far and wide through the intricate vanities and sordid cares of an everyday existence' (chs. 42, 9). Jermyn is a splendidly fresh character type, unanticipated in Marian's earlier novels, and the two scenes between him and the proud Mrs Transome in chapters 9 and 42 are scintillating. As she tells him at the end of the latter: 'If I sinned, my judgment went beforehand – that I should sin for a man like you'.

While never uninteresting and not without its distinctive felicities, *Felix Holt* dwindles into comparative insignificance when compared with its successor. *Middlemarch: A Study of Provincial Life* is Marian Evans' masterpiece and one of the classic works of nineteenth-century realistic fiction. Yet it is doubtful if Marian could have written the later novel without having written the earlier. *Felix Holt* was a preliminary attempt at a full-scale recreation of life in the northeast part of Loamshire (that is, Warwickshire) in the early 1830s, and a first attempt simultaneously to study both the determination of private life by public life and 'that mutual influence of dissimilar destinies which we shall see gradually unfolding itself'. The phrase is from the third chapter of the earlier novel. The equivalent statement in *Middlemarch* does not occur until chapter 11: 'any one watching keenly the stealthy convergence of human lots, sees a slow preparation of effects from one life on another, which tells like a calculated irony on the indifference or the frozen stare with which we look at our unintroduced neighbour'.

The most important way in which *Felix Holt* is a test run for *Middlemarch* concerns their central female characters. There is one such character in the earlier novel, Esther Lyon, who begins as a vessel of egotism preoccupied with her own pleasure but ends having developed altruistic and visionary capabilities and the humanistic equivalent of a religious sense. In the later novel this single character is split into two central female characters. It would seem that it was only by simplifying the character of Esther that Marian could create two enormously richer characters. The egotism and the self-regard are given to Rosamond Vincy, who marries the novel's equivalent of Harold Transome: both men are higher socially than the women they court and aware of their superior standing; both are competent or better in their chosen fields of worldly activity; but in their relationships with women, close scrutiny reveals the presence in both of an unreflecting male egotism that is the sign of a serious moral deficiency.

Esther's altruistic, visionary side is given to Dorothea Brooke. The stories of both young women are centrally concerned with the 'incalculable effect of one personality on another' (*Felix Holt*, ch. 22) and with knowledge through sorrow. When someone speaks to her of Saint Theresas and Elizabeth Frys, Esther remarks that a woman hardly ever has the opportunity to choose heroic activity as those figures did. A woman, she observes, is 'dependent on what happens to her. She must take meaner things, because only meaner things are within her reach' (ch. 27). This is exactly the subject raised in the 'Prelude' to *Middlemarch*, which opens with a reference to the same Saint Theresa of Avila, whose 'passionate, ideal nature demanded an epic life' and found one in sixteenth-century Spain, unlike the many Theresas born in later days who have found 'no epic life' for themselves and whose ardour has 'alternated between a vague ideal and the common yearning of womanhood'. For both Esther and Dorothea, the nineteenth-century equivalent of heroic action is the 'home epic' of marriage (*Middlemarch*, 'Finale'). The Felix Holt of the later novel is Will Ladislaw, who is less idealised but still a caricature of sentiment lacking in depth and subtlety. Many readers have found his and Dorothea's final coming together never more to part in chapter 83 to be one of the most unsatisfactory scenes in *Middlemarch*; but one is at least spared what is said of Esther and Felix in the comparable scene in chapter 45 of *Felix Holt*: he 'took her two hands between his, pressed together as children hold them up in prayer. Both of them felt too solemnly to be bashful. They looked straight into each other's eyes, as angels do when they tell some truth'.

Indications of the greater range and richness of *Middlemarch* are found within its text in the reflexive comments of the narrator on the work she is attempting to write. The world in which Dorothea Brooke lives precludes the possibility of heroic action for her; but this same world is the subject matter of the novel, and the narrator is keenly aware of the question of whether she is comparably precluded from writing a major imaginative work of epic or tragic dimensions – the two traditionally highest literary genres – in a modern prose idiom with realistic postulates. We have already seen it intimated that the modern equivalent of epic action is the 'home epic' of which marriage is the beginning and attraction and choice the prelude. 'Marriage is so unlike everything else', says Dorothea in chapter 81, 'There is something even awful in the nearness it brings'. But at the same time marriage is one of the repositories of the 'gentler emotions [that] will be ever new' that Marian spoke of in the 1848 letter in which she noted that in the nineteenth century the great literary subjects 'are used up, and civilization tends evermore to repress individual predominance, highly-wrought agony or ecstatic joy' (*L*, i, 247).

In other passages the narrator suggests that just as there is a modern form of epic action, so too there is a modern form of tragedy. In *Middlemarch* it is Lydgate, the aspiring medical researcher and husband of Rosamond Vincy, who is the subject of the modern tragedy. To recognise the tragic dimension in his story, the reader must learn not to find 'beneath his consideration' quotidian details like household expenses, house rent and life insurance and must learn to recognise the 'element of tragedy which lies in the very fact of frequency' (chs. 58, 20). To bring into focus this subtle process of 'gradual change' (ch. 15) that is cumulatively tragic, the narrator makes use of narratorial techniques and other fictional strategies similar to the techniques Lydgate himself uses in his scientific investigations. The virtuoso description in chapter 16 of the arduous invention that is Lydgate's ruling passion is at the same time a description of the creative method, and a celebration of the imaginative power, that informs and sustains *Middlemarch*:

> Fever had obscure conditions, and gave him that delightful labour of the imagination which is not mere arbitrariness, but the exercise of disciplined power – combining and constructing with the clearest eye for probabilities and the fullest obedience to knowledge; and then, in yet more energetic alliance with impartial Nature, standing aloof to invent tests by which to try its own work.
>
> Many men have been praised as vividly imaginative on the strength of their profuseness in indifferent drawing or cheap narration; . . . But these kinds of inspiration Lydgate regarded as rather vulgar and vinous compared with the imagination that reveals subtle actions inaccessible by any sort of lens, but tracked in that outer darkness through long pathways of necessary sequence by the inward light which is the last refinement of Energy, capable of bathing even the ethereal atoms in its ideally illuminated space. He for his part had tossed away all cheap inventions where ignorance finds itself able and at ease: he was enamoured of that arduous invention which is the very eye of research, provisionally framing its object and correcting it to more and more exactness of relation; he wanted to pierce the

obscurity of those minute processes which prepare human misery and joy, those invisible thoroughfares which are the first
lurking-places of anguish, mania, and crime, that delicate poise
and transition which determine the growth of happy or unhappy consciousness.

The operation of the author's scientific imagination is equally
well instanced in connection with the third major literary mode
that informs *Middlemarch*: that of narrative history. The narrator
refers to her work as provincial history and several times speaks of
herself as an historian. She is as much concerned to provide a
picture of human life that will lead to the amplification of experience (to recall phrases from 'The Natural History of German Life')
as were the narrators of the early George Eliot novels. Indeed, the
scope and detail of the picture presented in *Middlemarch* is greater
than that of any of her earlier novels, including *Romola*. 'I don't see
how I can leave anything out', Marian wrote to her publisher at
one point during the novel's composition, 'because I hope there is
nothing that will be seen to be irrelevant to my design, which is to
show the gradual action of ordinary causes rather than exceptional'
(*L*, v, 168). There are over a hundred characters in the novel,
including auctioneers, estate agents, horse dealers, veterinarians,
tenant farmers, superior and inferior gentry, pub keepers, grocers,
manufacturers, bankers, lawyers, clergymen and medical prac-
titioners, as well as their wives, children and servants. The novel's
several plot lines connect at innumerable points both with each
other and with the rest of the novel's world. The 'subtle movement' of 'old provincial society', the rise and decline of individuals
and families, the 'fresh threads of connection' gradually made
between municipal town and rural parish (ch. 11), are all copiously
detailed, as are the microcosmic reflections of some of the principal
forces that shaped the history of nineteenth-century Britain: the
coming of railroads, the movement for political reform, the reform
of the medical profession, the Evangelical revival and the supersession of distinctions of rank by those of class and the consequent
importance of vocational choice.

Henry James was impressed with the panoramic inclusiveness of
Middlemarch, but had reservations about the resultant 'diffuse-
ness'. 'If we write novels so', he wondered, 'how shall we write
History?' At the same time James spoke of the 'balanced contrast
between the two histories' of Lydgate and Dorothea as in itself

conveying 'that supreme sense of the vastness and variety of human life, under aspects apparently similar, which it belongs only to the greatest novels to produce' (*CH*, 359, 357). Within the comprehensive historical framework of *Middlemarch* is contained the richest moral and psychological explorations of character and motive in the George Eliot canon.

Dialogue, notation of externals, sententiae and the varieties of psychological omniscience are all utilised to the fullest and make for some of the most intensive and intelligent passages in nineteenth-century fiction. One example is the inside view of Dorothea in chapter 20, which registers the destabilising effect on her consciousness of both the city of Rome and her recent marriage, a passage that makes the often-praised meditative vigil of Isabel Archer in chapter 42 of James's *Portrait of a Lady* seem comparatively superficial and wordy. Another is also the masterful analysis of Casaubon's inner being in chapter 29, which lays bare his 'small hungry shivering self', and diagnoses his malaise as a deficiency in emotion, which manifests itself most pitifully in his shrinking from pity. A third example is the scenes between Lydgate and Rosamond, the novel's two most subtly realised characters, beginning with the early stages of their courtship, through the engagement scene, to chapter 58, when 'the terrible tenacity of this mild creature', and their 'total missing of each other's mental track' comes home to Lydgate, and finally to the great climactic scenes between them in chapters 64 and 65.

It is through these and other characterisations that the perennial thematic concerns of the George Eliot novels are memorably embodied. One is the belief that human good depends on the capacity for feeling – on the quality and breadth of emotion. The internal characteristic that is most determining of Lydgate's sorry lot is shown to be his 'spots of commonness', the 'unreflecting egoism' (chs. 15, 36) that for all his excellent intellectual and professional qualities reduce him to the same level of moral mediocrity as the altogether more gross and self-centred Harold Transome. Another is the belief in the terrible coercion of our deeds, which is seen in operation in the story of Bulstrode, who in one of the many splendid images in *Middlemarch* is described as feeling 'the scenes of his earlier life coming between him and everything else, as obstinately as when we look through the window from a lighted room, the objects we turn our backs on are still before us, instead of the grass and the trees' (ch. 61). Bulstrode's story also illustrates his creator's belief that 'there is no general doctrine which is not capable of eating out our morality if unchecked by the deep-seated habit of direct fellow-feeling with individual fellow-men' (ch. 61). Another belief concerns the mitigation of egotism and excessive self-concern through the recognition of an equivalent centre of self in others and of one's place in the commonalty of suffering. One thinks of Dorothea's night of introspection and suffering in chapter 80, followed by her dawn epiphany when she opens her curtains on an everyday scene of labour and endurance and feels herself a part of its 'involuntary, palpitating life'. The scene between her and Rosamond in the following chapter illustrates a final thematic concern with what may be called the humanistic economy of salvation, the 'saving influence of a noble nature, the divine efficacy of rescue that may lie in a self-subduing act of fellowship' (ch. 82).

Dorothea's night of sorrow and the scene between her and Rosamond were the two cited by F.W.H. Myers in a letter about *Middlemarch* that he wrote to Marian in December 1872. These scenes, he said, though they only existed on paper and in a book, were better 'than a ordinary passion', because they were 'the best conception of life that in this stage of the world we can form':

> Scenes like these go straight into the only imperishable world, – the world which is peopled by the lovely conceptions which have disengaged themselves in successive generations from the brains of men. The interest of such conceptions is more than artistic; they are landmarks in the history of the race, showing the height to which, at successive periods, man's ideal of his own life has vision.
>
> And you seem now to be the only person who can make life appear potentially noble and interesting without starting from any assumptions.
>
> (*L*, ix, 67–8)

This is all very Victorian; one inevitably recalls Matthew Arnold's belief that in the nineteenth century the power of philosophy and religion had waned and that 'more and more mankind will discover that we have to turn to poetry to interpret life for us, to console us, to sustain us'.[3] 'Poetry' was Arnold's synecdoche for great imaginative literature; but with his classical training and cultural biases it would never have occurred to him that the realistic novel of his day could have this power and efficacy. But Marian Evans conceived of her fiction in exactly this way, and in *Middlemarch* she produced a great work of imaginative literature that many readers since Myers have found a source of enlightenment, consolation and sustenance.

8

The 1870s / *Daniel Deronda* (1876)

That is how we see her during the latter years of her life: frail, delicate, shivering a little, much fatigued and considerably spent, but still meditating on what could be acquired and imparted; still living, in the intelligence, a freer, larger life than probably had ever been the portion of any woman.

Henry James

In August 1871, while at work on *Middlemarch*, Marian received the first of a series of extravagantly admiring letters from a thirty-year old Scot named Alexander Main. As her publisher reported after meeting the young man: 'He bears the mark of enthusiast about with him and you are his particular idol'. Lewes encouraged the correspondence because of its positive effect on what Marian described as her 'often-recurring hours of despondency which, after cramping my activity ever since I began to write, continue still to beset me with, I fear, a malign influence on my writing' (*L*, v, 207, 229). Before the year was out Main had sent her over twenty copiously effusive missives, in one of which he asked permission to prepare a volume of 'sayings' extracted from her works. Lewes and Marian liked the idea and at the end of the year the volume appeared under the title *Wise, Witty, and Tender Sayings in Prose and Verse, Selected from the Works of George Eliot*, with a dedication to the author 'in recognition of a genius as original as it is profound and a morality as pure as it is impassioned'. Two years later Marian was equally agreeable to the proposal for a second edition which would include selections from *Middlemarch*. But she was given pause by a statement in Main's draft preface concerning his compilation as compared with the works themselves:

Unless my readers are more moved towards the ends I seek by my works as wholes than by an assemblage of extracts, my

131

writings are a mistake. I have always exercised a severe watch against anything that could be called preaching, and if I have ever allowed myself in dissertation or in dialogue [anything] which is not part of the *structure* of my books, I have thereby sinned against my own laws . . . Unless I am condemned by my own principles, my books are not properly separable into 'direct' and 'indirect' teaching. My chief doubt as to the desirability of the 'Sayings' has always turned on the possibility that the volume might encourage such a view of my writings.

(*L*, v, 458–9)

The naivety of this statement is startling. In the same year Marian had written in another letter that her 'ideal' as an artist was 'to make matter and form an inseparable truthfulness' (*L*, v, 374). How could she not recognise the fundamental incompatibility between this creative ideal and a volume of extracted 'sayings'? How could she have countenanced the publication of such a volume at the very time she was deeply engaged creatively with *Middlemarch*?

It is clear that Marian's self-doubts and despondency created an insatiable need for reassurance that her writing was a force for good in the world. In the last decade of her life this need became linked with an autumnal solemnity and sibylline seriousness that was noted by many of those who came into contact with her. These qualities were on display on Sunday afternoons at the Priory, when visitors would one by one be taken over to Marian for a period of intense conversation. 'On Sunday', Dickens wryly wrote to Lewes in 1870, 'I hope to attend service at the Priory' (Haight, 453–4). And it was not only in her own home that Marian's gravitas was evident. The best known example is F.W.H. Myers's artful reminiscence of walking with her in the Fellows' Garden of Trinity College, Cambridge on a rainy evening in May 1873. It is an image of Marian Evans at her most Victorian:

she, stirred somewhat beyond her wont, and taking as her text the three words which have been used so often as the inspiring trumpet-calls of men, – the words *God, Immortality, Duty* – pronounced, with terrible earnestness, how inconceivable was the *first*, how unbelievable the *second*, and yet how peremptory and absolute the *third* . . . I listened, and night fell; her grave, majestic countenance turned toward me like a Sibyl's in the gloom; it was as though she withdrew from my grasp, one by one, the two scrolls of promise, and left me the third scroll only, awful with inevitable fates.[1]

The creative question that confronted Marian in the early 1870s must have been daunting: what does one write after *Middlemarch*? She did not know the answer in late 1871 when she confessed to being 'haunted by the fear that I am only saying again what I have already said in better fashion. For we all of us have our little store – our two or three beliefs which are the outcome of our character and experience'. There was a danger of 'harping' on them too long and the equally serious danger of taking up other beliefs that were not really one's own, 'but mere borrowing and echo'. Two years later the answer was finally becoming clear. In November 1873 she told her publisher that she was 'slowly simmering towards another big book'. Its composition was accompanied by the usual doubts and near despair; but work proceeded and by April 1875 Lewes could report to Blackwood that the novel was 'perfectly charming and all about English Ladies and Gentlemen and scene laid in Wiltshire', and that the title was *Daniel Deronda* (*L*, v, 212, 454,; vi, 136). Publication arrangements were decided upon later the same year; like *Middlemarch*, the new novel would appear not in the conventional three-volume format but in eight parts.

Daniel Deronda was an extraordinary departure for Marian Evans. There were of course the same quintessential 'two or three beliefs'; but there was much that was unprecedented in setting and subject matter, and in mode of presentation. Unlike all her previous works of fiction save *Romola*, Marian's seventh novel was not set in the Midlands; and unlike all of them it was not set in the past. For the seasoned reader of the George Eliot novels, it must have been initially startling to find the heroine of *Daniel Deronda* biding her time in a dreary railway station in 'Wessex' and reflecting on its dirt and shabbiness. Much of the action of the novel is set among the superior gentry of this region and there are a number of scenes of high life there, in London and on the continent. Even more unexpected are the novel's Jewish characters and settings. The reader is taken into the part of London inhabited by common Jews, including the shop of a pawnbroker and the living quarters of his family; there are samplings of Jewish life on the continent; and a great deal of information is provided about Jewish customs, lore, learning, history and nationalist aspirations. As Marian explained in a letter to Harriet Beecher Stowe, one of her intentions in *Deronda* was informative: to break down English 'stupidity' and prejudice concerning Jews, as well as the 'spirit of arrogance and contemptuous dictatorialness' that she regarded as a national disgrace (*L*, vi, 301–2).

The two plots of which *Deronda* is composed would have been less unfamiliar to readers of the George Eliot novels; but both contain distinctly new elements. The Jewish plot, which centres on the spiritual development of the title character, is Marian's most sustained and penetrating attempt to explore her longstanding interest in visionary experience, the possibilities of heroic action in the modern world, and the regenerating impact one human being can have on another. But there is no precedent for the extraordinary Jewish siblings who mediate his development: Mordecai, the consumptive visionary; and Mirah, a type of preternaturally virtuous poor child, the transcendent unreality of which in Dickens' novels Marian had condemned twenty years earlier in 'The Natural History of German Life'. The young Gwendolen Harleth is the focus of the gentile plot. Here there are a number of familiar elements: the marriage choice; egotism encountering a centre of self in others; the awful consequences of one's actions; and enlargement of life through suffering and sad experience. Gwendolen could well be described as a more sophisticated Esther Lyon or as an amalgam of Dorothea Brooke and Rosamond Vincy. On the other hand, the contemporary setting and the social world in which she moves make Gwendolen in some ways resemble these provincial heroines less than she does the title character of Tolstoy's contemporaneous *Anna Karenina*, or Isabel Archer, the heroine of Henry James' 1880 novel, *The Portrait of a Lady*, on which the influence of Marian's novel is patent.

The difference in *Deronda*'s mode of presentation as compared with its predecessors was the subject of R.E. Francillon's long review of the novel. To him it seemed 'practically a first book by a new author'. *Deronda* did not deal 'with the ordinary people who make up the actual world' or 'with the circumstances, events, characteristics, and passions that are common to us all'. The elaboration of such subjects was the provenance of the realistic novel; *Deronda* was different in kind. Its 'conception, scope, circumstance, and form' separated it from the earlier George Eliot novels. In fact, it was not really a novel at all, but a romance or, more precisely 'a direct, uncompromising adaptation of the spirit and form of the romance to a novel of our own time'. It did not grapple with fact, but with 'the higher and wider truths'. Deronda's story was wholly idealised while the subject of the Gwendolen plot was 'the birth of a human soul'; she was 'as much a romance heroine as Undine' – the title character of Fouqué's tale about a water sprite who marries a knight and thereby acquires a human soul (CH, 382–98).

Up to a point, Francillon's commentary is excellent. He is right to insist on the inappositeness of realistic conventions in bringing much of Deronda into focus and in pointing up romance elements and continental analogues. But his comments on the Gwendolen plot need to be qualified. There are important generic differences between the novel's two story lines, and Gwendolen's has all the essential elements of the typical marriage plot of the earlier George Eliot novels. The principal creative challenge Marian faced in the novel was not that of adopting the form of the realistic novel to romance imperatives, but that of accommodating and making interactive a realistic plot and a romance plot.

In chapter 46 the narrator remarks that 'the romantic or unusual in real life requires some adaptation'. The attempt to make the required adaptations is responsible for some of the less satisfactory features of the novel. The remark is made with reference to the Meyrick family, which is Mirah's point of entry into the gentile world. The cosy Chelsea home of Mrs Meyrick and her three daughters positively glows with Gemütlichkeit and resembles nothing so much as a sentimentalised Dickensian hearth. The equivalent in the other plot is the home of the pawnbroker Cohen and his family, which is Deronda's point of entry into the Jewish world. The family is realistically rendered (as is Mirah's father Lapidoth), and the notations of Jewish low life do provide a counterweight to Mirah and Mordecai, who are idealised types of Jewish nobility. But there is a seen-from-the-outside caricatural aspect to the Cohens that makes them the opposite equals of the Meyricks.

These adaptations are only two of a number of ways in which Marian tried to bind together her novel's disparate parts. It is not hard to see what she meant when she said that she intended 'everything in the book to be related to everything else there' (L, vi, 290). But this is not to say that she was successful in realising her intention. Numerous commentators have found the two plots to be qualitatively dissimilar and otherwise immiscible. F.R. Leavis' 1960 discussion is the best known statement of his view. For him the

Gwendolen half of *Deronda* is superb and shows the author's greatness 'at its most Tolstoyan'. The rendering was 'superlatively successful' and nothing less than the greatest achievement of 'the born novelist, possessed by her themes and in full possession of them', drawing on a wealth of 'relevant experience and observation'. In contrast, 'the Jewish part was – inevitably – done from the outside'. It was the product of the same strictly intellectual energies that had gone into the working up of *Romola*. At its centre there was 'an unreduced enclave of immaturity'. The attempt to dramatise the 'dubiously emotional and idealistic impulses' of Deronda could produce only unreality. He was 'a mere emotionalized postulate'.[2]

Few would disagree with the kind of praise Leavis lavished on the Gwendolen part of the novel. The heroine is superbly conceived and superbly characterised. This 'poor spoiled child with the lovely lips and eyes and the majestic figure' has a naive delight in herself and a consciousness filled with a sense of her superior claims on life. With her spontaneous sense of capability, 'inborn energy of egoistic desire', and youthful self-exaltation, she feels herself well-equipped for mastery of life. All of this is brilliantly conveyed, as is the 'iridescence of her character – the play of various, nay, contradictory tendencies', including 'a certain fierceness of maidenhood' (chs. 26, 4, 7).

Gwendolen wants to escape the humdrum and live with intensity, but for all her gifts she lacks two key constituents of being: she has no religious sense or habits of thought and feeling; and she has no roots. While at work on *Deronda* Marian had written to a correspondent concerning the former, urging her 'to consider your early religious experience as a portion of valid knowledge, and to cherish its emotional results in relation to objects and ideas which are either substitutes or metamorphoses of the earlier' (*L*, vi, 120). But Gwendolen has none of this valid knowledge from which her adult self can derive support. Nor has she any of its secular equivalent. Speaking of the deficiencies of her childhood in chapter 3, the narrator reiterates one of the author's deepest beliefs: that a human life 'should be well rooted in some spot of a native land, where it may get the love of tender kinship for the face of earth, the labours men go forth to . . . a spot where the definiteness of early memories may be inwrought with affection, and kindly acquaintance with all neighbours . . . may spread not by sentimental effort and reflection, but as a sweet habit of the blood'.

As a result, when at the age of twenty-one Gwendolen is asked what she would like to do with her life, she can only respond 'flightily' and is 'at a loss to give an answer of deeper origin'. Her favourite key to life is simply doing as she likes. She does realise that it will be necessary for her to marry; but the horizon of her expectation is supplied only by 'genteel romance', which gives her 'about as accurate a conception of marriage . . . as she had of magnetic currents and the law of storms' (chs. 7, 6, 27). Nothing in her experience or reading has prepared her for Grandcourt, a fastidious gentleman whose 'refined negations' (ch. 54) she finds attractive. Her crucial moment of choice comes in the engagement scene in chapter 27, during which the reader is allowed to see what Gwendolen cannot: that Grandcourt's strongest wish during their interview is 'to be completely master of this creature'. It is only after her marriage that Gwendolen comes to see that her husband's refined negations are the outward sign not of a superior sensibility but of the 'barrenness of a fastidious egoism'. Grandcourt's is a 'negative mind . . . as diffusive as fog, clinging to all objects and spoiling all contact'; and Gwendolen soon realises that in uniting her life with his she has become a subject in 'her husband's empire of fear' (chs. 25, 48, 35).

It is not as easy to agree with Leavis' dismissal of Deronda as a mere emotionalised postulate rooted in his creator's residual immaturity. Not that there can be any doubt he is an idealised romance figure. 'If you like', the narrator admits in chapter 41, 'he was romantic': his 'young energy and spirit of adventure' recall 'the world-wide legends of youthful heroes going to seek the hidden tokens of their birth and its inheritance of tasks'. Deronda's eyes are associated with those of Dante's *spiriti magni*, and his face with that of Christ in a Titian painting. And his inner qualities of a Christlike nature are repeatedly underlined: his 'fervour of sympathy . . . on behalf of others' and 'hatred of all injury'; his 'habitual disposition' to admit the claims of others; and his 'precious seeing' that bathes 'all objects in a solemnity as of a sunset-glow' and is 'begotten of a loving reverential emotion' (chs. 16, 40, 47).

It is just as obvious that there is a schematic cast to the Deronda plot that relates to the familiar Victorian concerns with Vocation and Duty, and with escaping both the external pressure of the 'hard unaccommodating Actual' (ch. 33) and the internal circumscription of miserable aims that end in self. This feature of the Deronda plot is much too diagrammatic to be compelling art, and

pales in comparison with Gwendolen's realistically rendered encounter with the Actual without and the egotistic self within. But
this is not the only, and not the most important, feature of the
Deronda plot. The key criterion for assessing this half of the novel
is the extent to which Deronda's quintessential qualities are made
psychologically convincing. Romance stylisation is the inevitable
concomitant of the two essentially religious subjects that are at the
core of the Deronda plot: the origin and nature of his visionary
disposition and Christlike temperament; and the mode of operation of his redeeming influence on others. The former is explored
through the narrator's powers of psychological omniscience; the
latter through the copiously detailed stages of Deronda's relationship with Gwendolen, which is the central thread in the novel
from its opening to its closing page.

Marian's sense of the difficulty of her undertaking is signalled
within the text by the two striking scientific images in the reflexive
epigraphs to chapters 1 and 16. Both refer elliptically to the difficulty of threading 'the hidden pathways of feeling and thought' in
attempting to reach the deepest levels – the origin or 'true beginning' – of Deronda's being. The opening paragraph of the first
chapter, following the epigraph, immediately places the reader
inside Deronda's mind and reports on his reaction to first setting
eyes on Gwendolen; while the other epigraph is followed by an
extended flashback to a crucial inner moment in his adolescence. It
is a good example of the psychological depths the narrator reaches
as well as of the limitations of her exploration. Chapter 16 attempts
to show through an extended passage of retrospective psychological omniscience that the originating moment of Deronda's sense of
difference – of his being set apart from others – occurs when he
comes to suspect at the age of thirteen that he is illegitimate and
that there is a secret concerning his birth. This suspicion gives him
'something like a new sense in relation to all the elements of his
life'. The sense is of 'an entailed disadvantage' which, like a
deformed foot, 'makes a restlessly active spiritual yeast' and can
lead to a person's becoming estranged from his fellow human
beings. But with Deronda this felt deprivation is said to make his
imagination 'tender', give rise to 'premature reflection on certain
questions of life', and impart a bias or susceptibility towards the
sorrows and pains of others.

The analysis in this chapter is impressive and largely persuasive;
but at one point the narrator attributes Deronda's exceptional reac-

tion to his sense of loss to some antecedent 'inborn lovingness . . . strong enough to keep itself level with resentment'. Here the reader again seems at a distance from the origin of Deronda's inner being, for the narrator does not explore the question of the source of this inborn quality or of why Deronda possesses it whereas most persons are like Gwendolen in entering the world with 'an inborn energy of egoistic desire' (ch. 4). The narratorial attempts in chapters 17 and 41 to account for the origin of Deronda's sense of Jewishness and the special affinity he feels first to Mirah and then to Mordecai are equally penetrating and equally leave difficult questions unanswered (as does the unmentioned matter of Deronda's putative circumcision[3]).

The dramatisation and analysis of the 'religious' aspect of the Deronda–Gwendolen relationship is more satisfying. Deronda is drawn to her, as he is to others, because of his sense of the possibility of 'telling upon their lives with some sort of redeeming influence'. But in Gwendolen's case there is 'something beyond his habitual compassionate fervour – something due to the fascination of her womanhood' (chs. 28). E.S. Shaffer has rightly emphasised the implicit sexual element in their relationship.[4] It is part of the 'hidden affinity' Gwendolen senses between them and part of 'the hold Deronda had from the first taken on her mind'. But there is also something beyond 'personal love' in the attraction; and it is in the eventual disentangling of these strands that much of the interest in this relationship lies (chs. 29, 35, 63).

By chapter 35 Gwendolen has realised that Deronda is unique among the men that she knows and that 'in some mysterious way he is becoming a part of her conscience'. The narrator suggests that this inner presence may be helping to precipitate 'that change of mental poise which has been fitly named conversion'. The next chapter ends with the impressive scene between them in the library of a country house which is 'as warmly odorous as a private chapel in which the censers have been swinging'. Here Deronda speaks of 'the higher, the religious life' as a refuge from personal troubles, appetites and vanities; Gwendolen looks 'startled and thrilled as by an electric shock'; and crucifixion imagery (piercing) is first used. But Deronda's words are not efficacious. In chapter 48 Gwendolen laments that she is unable to alter her inner life despite her desire to do so; and Deronda is unable to see how he can 'grasp the long-growing process of this young creature's wretchedness . . . how arrest and change it with a sentence'.

Their next two interviews take place in Genoa in the time immediately after Grandcourt's death, when Gwendolen is consumed with remorse and feelings of guilt. In essence these chapters are a repetition of the situation in chapter 19 of *Mr. Gilfil's Love Story*, written almost twenty years earlier, in which through Maynard's ministrations Caterina finally unburdens herself of her guilt-ridden feelings concerning the death of Wybrow. In the earlier work Christian reassurance concerning God's love for all his creatures is efficacious, and is fortified by a bond of love rooted in childhood that is soon to culminate in marriage; confessor and penitent are also lover and beloved. In *Deronda* the situation is much more complicated. The imagery of piercing is again deployed and their are other Christian allusions; but their reference is not to the Christian God but to Deronda's Christ-like love for a tormented soul. For his love to become efficacious, it must be disengaged from sexual or personal love, a task no less easy to effect psychologically than to render artistically.

The disengagement is not effected until their final meeting in chapter 69. Four chapters earlier Deronda's words concerning Gwendolen's potential to be among 'the best of women, such as make others glad that they are born' had been – again Christian imagery is employed – 'like the touch of a miraculous hand' to her and had brought 'a strength that seemed like the beginning of a new existence'; but an existence that seemed inseparable from Deronda's. In the final meeting his words concern his discovery of his Jewishness and his plans to marry Mirah and go to the East to help make his people a nation again. For the first time in her life Gwendolen is 'dislodged from her supremacy in her own world' and feels the pressure of 'a vast mysterious movement' – and a tremor 'deeper than personal jealousy' that gives her the felt sense of a larger existence beyond self. It is the equivalent of Dorothea's epiphany in chapter 80 of *Middlemarch*; for both young women the electric shocks of passion are succeeded by the 'waves' of suffering and sorrowful remembrance. And so, while Deronda goes east to a life of possibly heroic activity, Gwendolen retires into provincial obscurity to build on the valid religious knowledge he has imparted to her and belatedly to develop the sweet habits of other-regarding activity that will help make others glad that they were born. The redemptive process through which she is guided by Deronda's disinterested love is protracted, its stages seem at times excessively detailed, and they are accompanied by commentary that at times might well be called preaching. But the redeeming influence of one human being on another is impressively rendered, and it is the principal means through which the two generically different plots of Marian's last and in some ways most ambitious novel are powerfully related to each other.

When the last monthly instalment of *Daniel Deronda* appeared in September 1876 Marian had a little over four years to live and Lewes a little over two. There was to be a two-part answer to the question of what was left to write after one had written *Daniel Deronda*: the beginnings of an eighth novel worked on during 1877; and a collection of essays, *Impressions of Theophrastus Such*, published in 1879. In the abandoned novel, Marian returned to the part of the Midlands she called Loamshire and to the early nineteenth-century past – the Napoleonic period between the turn of the century, the time of *Adam Bede* and *Silas Marner*, and the late 1820s and early 1830s, in which *Scenes of Clerical Life*, *The Mill on the Floss*, *Felix Holt* and *Middlemarch* are all set.

In the novel's opening paragraph, time and place are evoked with the familiar copiousness of notation and direct address to the latter-day reader that had been missing from *Deronda*. There is a certain amount of initial throat-clearing, but the narrator is soon caught up in her retrospect and struggling to control her abundant materials:

> This story will take you if you please into Central England and into what have been often called the Good old times. It is a telescope you may look through a telephone you may put your ear to: but there is no compulsion. If you only care about the present fashions in dress & talk in politics and religion pass on without offence as you would pass the man with the telescope in the Place de la Concorde, not mounting to look through his lenses and then abusing him because he does not show you something less distant and more to your taste than the aspects of the heavenly bodies. Allow those who like it to interest themselves in the sad or joyous fortunes of people who saw the beginning of the Times newspaper, trembled or felt defiant at the name of Buonoparte, defended bull baiting, were excited by the writing of Cobbett and submitted to some invisible power which ordained that their black waist buttons should be nine inches higher than those of their Fathers. These people did not

manage the land well; they knew little about subsoils and top dressings, allowed trees and hedgerows to take title of their acres & in all ways helped the weather to make bad harvests. But their farming was picturesque & it suited the preservation of game. A large population of hares partridges & pheasants had short but let us hope merry lives between the times when they were made war on by the superior race who intervened between them & the unscrupulous foxes that would have killed & eaten them without ulterior views. And as many foxes [as] were allowed to remain & enjoy their known pleasure in being hunted were handsomely provided with covers. It was a bosky beautiful landscape that was to be seen almost everywhere in our rich Central plain, when a little rise of ground gave the horseman a possibility of seeing over a stretch of tree-studded hedgerows enclosing here & there the long roofs of a homestead & merging in woods which gave a wide-spread hint of the landowner's mansion hidden with its park & pools & resounding rookery far away from the vulgar gaze.[5]

Another notebook entry introduces Cyril Ambrose, 'a man of inventive power in science as well as philosophy' who has married young and is very poor, and a Mr Rastin, a double agent working for both the French and the English.[6] There are intimations of high-society intrigue involving London aristocrats and a masquerade; but there is also material concerning a dispute over school revenues in a midland town. It is unclear how the novel would have developed; but there is enough of interest to make one regret that Marian turned her attention to the volume of essays.

Like the unfinished novel, there is a 'looking backward' cast to the *Impressions of Theophrastus Such*. One example is that at the end of her writing career Marian returns to the form of the moral essay that she had used in 'Poetry and Prose, from the Notebook of an Eccentric', a cluster of brief pieces that appeared in the Coventry *Herald and Observer* in the mid-1840s. Another model for the *Impressions* were the character sketches of Theophrastus and those of his seventeenth-century French imitator Jean de la Bruyère – both of whom exemplify what the narrator of the *Impressions* describes as 'loving laughter' and the 'delightful power which . . . depends on a discrimination only compatible with the varied sensibilities which give sympathetic insight'. Of the eighteen essays, a number describe character types (for example, 'A Too

Deferential Man' and 'A Man Surprised at his own Originality'), while others are given over to the discussion of moral qualities and such literary issues as plagiarism, burlesque and originality. The most personal essay is 'Looking Backward', in which *encore une fois* Marian evokes the provincial England of her early years.

The overall impression made by the *Impressions* is one of tediousness; it is the result of the author's failure to create an engaging persona. As he describes himself in the opening essay, 'Looking Inward', Theophrastus Such is a confirmed bachelor and would-be author whose one published work, a humorous romance, was a failure except in the Cherokee translation, 'where the jokes are rendered with all the serious eloquence characteristic of the red races'. His innocent vanity of desiring to be agreeable is complicated by his habit of critical scrutiny of others; but 'if I laugh at you, O fellow-men . . . Dear blunderers, I am one of you'. Half an hour of the post-prandial loquacity, periphrastic self-consciousness and genteel witticisms of this narrator is enough to send one back to *The Spanish Gypsy* with a sense of relief. As early as 1902, Leslie Stephen could 'hardly believe that anyone now read [the *Impressions*] except from a sense of duty'.[7]

Lewes sent the manuscript of *Impressions of Theophrastus Such* to Blackwood in November 1878. A week later he died. He had been in bad health for some time and the shadow of inevitable parting had fallen across his and Marian's union at least since the mid-1870s. She was initially devastated by her loss and remained in seclusion for some time. Among the works with which she consoled herself was *In Memoriam*, described long before as enshrining 'the highest tendency of this age . . . the sanctification of human love as a religion' (*WR*, 64 [1855], 597). Another was the unfinished third volume of Lewes' *Problems of Life and Mind*, which Marian took it upon herself to prepare for publication. And in the summer of 1879 she began rereading *The Divine Comedy* with John Walter Cross, a family friend and financial advisor twenty years her junior.

As the summer progressed Marian and Cross found themselves becoming increasingly intimate. In late August she noted in her diary that a 'decisive conversation' between them had taken place. The following April Marian complained to a close friend that she was 'tired of being set on a pedestal and expected to vent wisdom' (Haight, 528, 537). The next month she and Cross were married; the ceremony was held not in a Unitarian setting or a registrar's office, but in an Anglican church. A number of friends who had stood by Marian during the quarter century of her legally and ecclesiastically unsanctioned union with Lewes were taken aback by her conventional behaviour. But at least her brother was pleased. Marian had informed Isaac's solicitor of her marriage and for the first time since 1857 he communicated with her in order to express his best wishes. In her reply Marian spoke of her 'never broken . . . affection for you which began when we were little ones', and of the only point to be regretted in her marriage – 'that I am much older that he' (*L*, vii, 287).

The happiness of Mr and Mrs Cross was not to be longlasting. In June, during their wedding trip to Italy, Cross experienced some kind of mental derangement in Venice which culminated in his leaping from the balcony of their hotel room into the Grand Canal. And before the year was out Marian became seriously ill. She died three days before Christmas. 'Tell them I have great pain in the left side' were her last words (Cross, iii, 349). There was opposition to the proposal that she be buried in Westminster Abbey and the body was interred in an unconsecrated part of Highgate Cemetery close by the grave of Lewes.

After her death, Cross devoted himself to the preparation of a life of his wife. It appeared in three volumes in 1885 under the title *George Eliot's Life as Related in her Letters and Journals*. It was not a conventional biography but, as Cross described it in his preface, a form of autobiography made up of extracts from Marian's letters and journals chronologically arranged 'to show the development of her intellect and character'. This rationale led to the editorial deletion of much that was personal, intimate and colourful. A small but telling example is the omission of the three italicised words from Marian's account of how she first came to write fiction: 'one morning as I was *lying in bed*, thinking what should be the subject of my first story, my thoughts merged themselves into a dreamy doze, and I imagined myself writing a story of which the title was – "The Sad Fortunes of the Reverend Amos Barton." I was soon wide awake again, and told G.' (*L*, ii, 407).

Gladstone complained that Cross's compilation was 'not a Life at all. It is a Reticence in three volumes' (*L*, i, xiv). And when Margaret Oliphant read the *Life*, she was led to reflect that its subject 'must have been a dull woman with a great genius distinct from herself, something like the gift of the old prophets, which they sometimes exercised with only a dim sort of perception of what it meant . . . She took herself with tremendous seriousness, that is evident, and was always on duty, never relaxing, her letters ponderous beyond description'.[8] But William Hale White (Mark Rutherford) knew better. He had known Marian well in the early 1850s when they were both living in Chapman's house, and when he read the *Life* he wrote to the *Athenaeum* to correct the impression produced by Cross, who had made her too 'respectable'. In doing so White left an image of Marian Evans that is an excellent counterbalance to Myers' sombre picture of the sibyl of the Trinity Fellows' Garden and other accounts and impressions of the famous Victorian novelist and cultural prophet in the closing decade of her life:

> She was really one of the most sceptical, unusual creatures I ever knew, and it was this side of her character which to me was the most attractive. She told me that it was worth while to undertake all the labour of learning French if it resulted in nothing more than reading one book – Rousseau's 'Confessions.' That saying was perfectly symbolical of her, and reveals more completely what she was, at any rate in 1851–54, than page after page of attempt on my part at critical analysis. I can see her now, with her hair over her shoulders, the easy chair half sideways to the fire, her feet over the arms, and a proof in her hands, in that dark room at the back of No. 142, and I confess I hardly recognize her in the pages of Mr. Cross's – on many accounts – most interesting volumes. I do hope that in some future edition, or in some future work, the salt and spice will be restored to the records of George Eliot's entirely unconventional life. As the matter now stands, she has not had full justice done to her, and she has been removed from the class – the great and noble church, if I may so call it – of the Insurgents, to one more genteel, but certainly not so interesting.[9]

Notes

Chapter 1

1. *The Industrial Revolution in Coventry* (Oxford: Oxford UP, 1960), 11, 145. For information about Coventry in the early 1830s I have drawn on Prest and on Alice Lynes, *George Eliot's Coventry*, Coventry & North Warwickshire History Pamphlets, No. 6 (Coventry Historical Association, 1970).
2. *An Inquiry concerning the Origin of Christianity*, 3rd edition (London: Trübner, 1870), v–vi, 372, 375, 376–7.
3. Howard R. Murphy, 'The Ethical Revolt against Christian Orthodoxy in Early Victorian England', *American Historical Review*, 60 (1955), 801, 816.
4. *Inquiry*, xiii.
5. *The Life of Jesus Critically Examined*, trans. George Eliot, 4th edition (London: Swan Sonnenschein, 1902), 65, 757, 780–1.
6. Waldo Hilary Dunn, *James Anthony Froude: A Biography* (Oxford: Clarendon, 1961), i, 236.
7. William J. Brazill, *The Young Hegelians* (New Haven: Yale UP, 1970), 105.
8. *An Autobiography* (London: Williams & Norgate, 1904), i, 396.
9. Raymond Chapman and Eleanora Gottlieb, 'A Russian View of George Eliot', *Nineteenth-Century Fiction*, 33 (1978), 352.

Chapter 2

1. *An Autobiography*, i, 394–5.
2. *Athenaeum*, 8 December 1894, 790.
3. *The Earlier Letters of John Stuart Mill 1812–1848*, ed. Francis E. Mineka (Toronto: U of Toronto P; London: Routledge & Kegan Paul, 1963), 499; *Jane Welsh Carlyle: Letters to her Family, 1839–1863*, ed. Leonard Huxley (London: John Murray, 1924), 319–20.
4. *Letters to her Family*, 329.
5. Frederick Engels, *Ludwig Feuerbach and the Outcome of Classical German Philosophy* (New York: International Publishers, 1941), 18, 25.
6. *The Essence of Christianity*, [trans. Marian Evans] (New York: Harper Torchbooks, 1957), xxxvii, 275, 48, 264–5, 268, 271.
7. 'The Lesson of Balzac', *Literary Criticism: French Writers, Other European Writers, The Prefaces to the New York Edition*, ed. Leon Edel (New York: Library of America, 1984), 125–6.
8. *The Portable Nietzsche*, ed. Walter Kaufmann (New York: Viking, 1954), 515.

Chapter 3

1. *The Works of John Ruskin*, Library edition, ed. E.T. Cook and Alexander

Wedderburn (London: George Allen, 1903–12), iii, 85; i, 421; v, 63, 32.
2. *Old Goriot*, trans. Marion Ayton Crawford (Harmondsworth: Penguin, 1951), 150.

Chapter 4

1. Suzanne Graver, *George Eliot and Community: A Study in Social Theory and Fictional Form* (Berkeley: U of California P, 1984), 14.
2. John Goode, '*Adam Bede*', in *Critical Essays on George Eliot*, ed. Barbara Hardy (London: Routledge & Kegan Paul, 1970), 19.
3. *Essays on Literature: American Writers, English Writers*, ed. Leon Edel (New York: Library of America, 1984), 914.
4. Fred Kaplan, *Thomas Carlyle: A Biography* (Ithaca, New York: Cornell UP, 1983), 100.
5. 'The Knowable Community in George Eliot's Novels', *Novel: A Forum on Fiction*, 2 (1969), 265–6.
6. I am indebted to Robyn R. Warhol, 'Toward a Theory of the Engaging Narrator: Earnest Interventions in Gaskell, Stowe, and Eliot', *PMLA*, 101 (1986), 811–8. Also see W.H. Harvey's 'The Ominiscient Author Convention', in his *The Art of George Eliot* (London: Chatto & Windus, 1961), 64–89.
7. *Essays on Literature*, 921.

Chapter 5

1. 'Repression and Vocation in George Eliot: A Review Essay', *Women and Literature*, 7 (1979), 3.
2. *George Sand and the Victorians: Her Influence and Reputation in Nineteenth-Century England* (New York: Columbia UP, 1977), 158.
3. '*Armgart* – George Eliot on the Woman Artist', *Victorian Poetry*, 18 (1980), 79.
4. 'The Greening of Sister George', *Nineteenth-Century Fiction*, 35 (1980), 299.
5. 'George Eliot's "Life"', *Nineteenth-Century*, 17 (1885), 476.
6. Sandra M. Gilbert and Susan Gubar, *The Madwoman in the Attic: The Woman Writer and the Nineteenth-Century Literary Imagination* (New Haven: Yale UP, 1979), 492; Elizabeth Showalter, *A Literature of their Own: British Women Novelists from Brontë to Lessing* (Princeton: Princeton UP, 1977), 127.
7. *D.H. Lawrence: A Personal Record*, 2nd edition, ed. J.D. Chambers (London: Cass, 1965), 97–8.
8. *The Teaching of George Eliot* (Leicester: Leicester UP, 1984), 65–6.
9. *The Diary of Henry Crabb Robinson*, ed. Derek Hudson (London: Oxford UP, 1967), 306.
10. '*The Mill on the Floss*', in *Critical Essays on George Eliot*, 45, 50.

Chapter 6

1. 'George Eliot', *Collected Essays* (London: Hogarth, 1966), i, 201.

2. Sir Walter Scott, *The Prefaces to the Waverley Novels*, ed. Mark A. Weinstein (Lincoln: U of Nebraska P, 1978), 34–7.
3. 'Romola as Fable', *Critical Essays on George Eliot*, 83, 85, 93.
4. 'George Eliot in the 1860's', *Victorian Studies*, 5 (1961), 96–7.
5. Engels, 25, 27, 29.
6. *Auguste Comte and Positivism* (Ann Arbor: U of Michigan P, 1961), 134–5, 138–9. On this and other aspects of Comte's thought, also see T.R. Wright, *The Religion of Humanity: The Impact of Comtean Positivism on Victorian Britain* (Cambridge: Cambridge UP, 1986).
7. On the influence of experimental science on the later novels, see Sally Shuttleworth, *George Eliot and Nineteenth-Century Science: The Make-Believe of a Beginning* (Cambridge: Cambridge UP, 1984).
8. *Essays on Literature*, 943, 957.

Chapter 7

1. 'Felix Holt the Radical', *Critical Essays on George Eliot*, 101, 107, 108, 113.
2. 'Introduction' to his edition of *Felix Holt* (Harmondsworth: Penguin, 1972), 38.
3. 'The Study of Poetry', *Essays in Criticism*, second series, ed. R.S. Littlewood (London: Macmillan, 1960), 2.

Chapter 8

1. 'George Eliot', *Essays Modern* (London: Macmillan, 1897), 269.
2. 'George Eliot's Zionist Novel', *Commentary*, 30 (1960), 317, 321–2, 318–21.
3. See K.M. Newton, 'Daniel Deronda and Circumcision', *Essays in Criticism*, 31 (1981), 313–27.
4. 'Daniel Deronda and the Conventions of Fiction', in her 'Kubla Khan' and 'The Fall of Jerusalem': The Mythological School in Biblical Criticism and Secular Literature 1770–1880 (Cambridge: Cambridge UP, 1975), 256f.
5. William Baker, 'A New George Eliot Manuscript', in *George Eliot: Centenary Essays and an Unpublished Fragment*, ed. Anne Smith (London: Vision, 1980), 10–11.
6. Jerome Beaty, 'George Eliot's Notebook for an Unwritten Novel', *Princeton University Library Chronicle*, 18 (1957), 175–82.
7. *George Eliot* (New York: Macmillan, 1902), 195.
8. *The Autobiography and Letters of Mrs. M.O.W. Oliphant*, ed. Mrs. Harry Coghill (New York: Dodd, Mead, 1899), 7.
9. *Athenaeum*, 28 November 1885, 702.

Further Reading

Primary Works

(a)   Works Published during the Author's Life

Good editions of the seven George Eliot novels, and of *Scenes of Clerical Life*, are available in the Penguin English Library; some are also available in the Oxford World's Classics. The two volumes of verse and *Impressions of Theophrastus Such* are included in the various collected editions of the works of George Eliot, as are the two pieces of shorter fiction, 'The Lifted Veil' and 'Brother Jacob'. Marian Evans's translation of Strauss, *The Life of Jesus Critically Examined*, has been reprinted (London: SCM, 1972), as has her translation of Feuerbach's *Essence of Christianity* (New York: Harper Torchbooks, 1957).

(b)   Other Writings

Essays. Ed. Thomas Pinney. London: Routledge & Kegan Paul/New York: Columbia UP, 1963. An appendix lists all of the periodical essays and reviews.
A Writer's Notebook 1854–1879 and Uncollected Writings. Ed. Joseph Wisenfarth. Charlottesville: UP of Virginia, 1981. Includes a number of pieces not in Pinney.
Letters. Ed. Gordon S. Haight. 9 vols. New Haven: Yale UP, 1954–78.

Secondary Works

(a)   Bibliographies

Fulmer, Constance Marie, *George Eliot: A Reference Guide*. Boston: G.K. Hall, 1977. Annotated list of reviews, articles and books from 1858 to 1971.
Higdon, David Leon, 'A Bibliography of George Eliot Criticism 1971–77', *Bulletin of Bibliography* 37 (1980): 90–103.
Knoepflmacher, U.C., 'George Eliot', *Victorian Fiction: A Second Guide to Research*. Ed. George H. Ford. New York: Modern Language Association, 1978. 234–73.
Levine, George, *An Annotated Critical Bibliography of George Eliot*. New York: St. Martin's Press, 1988.

(*b*) Biographies

Cross, J.W., *George Eliot's Life as Related in her Letters and Journals*. 3 vols. Edinburgh/London: Blackwood, 1885. Often reprinted in collected editions of the works of George Eliot.
Haight, Gordon S., *George Eliot: A Biography*. Oxford: Clarendon, 1968. The standard life.
Laski, Marghanita, *George Eliot and her World*. London: Thames & Hudson/ New York: Scribner's, 1973. Excellent short account of the life, with many illustrations.
Redinger, Ruby V., *George Eliot: The Emergent Self*. New York: Knopf, 1975/London: Bodley Head, 1976.

(*c*) General Studies and Monographs

Ashton, Rosemary, *George Eliot*. Past Masters. Oxford: Oxford UP, 1983.
Auster, Henry, *Local Habitations: Regionalism in the Early Novels of George Eliot*. Cambridge, MA: Harvard UP, 1970.
Barrett, Dorothea, *Vocation and Desire: George Eliot's Heroines*. London: Routledge, 1989.
Beer, Gillian, *George Eliot*. Key Women Writers. Brighton: Harvester, 1986.
Bennett, Joan, *George Eliot: Her Mind and Art*. Cambridge: Cambridge UP, 1948.
Dentith, Simon, *George Eliot*. Brighton: Harvester, 1986.
Dodd, Valerie A., *George Eliot: An Intellectual Life*. London: Macmillan, 1990. Intellectual development to 1856.
Gilbert, Sandra M. and Susan Gubar, *The Madwoman in the Attic: The Woman Writer and the Nineteenth-Century Literary Imagination*. New Haven: Yale UP, 1979, 443–535.
Hardy, Barbara, *The Novels of George Eliot: A Study in Form*. London: Athlone, 1959.
Hardy, Barbara, *Particularities: Readings in George Eliot*. London: Peter Owen, 1982.
Harvey, W.J., *The Art of George Eliot*. London: Chatto & Windus, 1961.
Knoepflmacher, U.C., *George Eliot's Early Novels: The Limits of Realism*. Berkeley: U of California P, 1968.
Leavis, F.R., *The Great Tradition: George Eliot, Henry James, Joseph Conrad*. London: Chatto & Windus, 1948. 28–125.
Mann, Karen B., *The Language that Makes George Eliot's Fiction*. Baltimore: Johns Hopkins UP, 1983.
Milner, Ian, *The Structure of Values in George Eliot*. Prague: Universita Karlova, 1968.
Mintz, Alan, *George Eliot and the Novel of Vocation*. Cambridge, MA: Harvard UP, 1978.
Myers, William, *The Teaching of George Eliot*. Leicester: Leicester UP, 1984.
Newton, K.M., *George Eliot, Romantic Humanist: A Study of the Philosophical Structure of her Novels*. London: Macmillan, 1981.

Paris, Bernard J., *Experiments in Life: George Eliot's Quest for Values*. Detroit: Wayne State UP, 1965.

Roberts, Neil, *George Eliot: Her Beliefs and her Art*. London: Elek, 1975.

Shuttleworth, Sally, *George Eliot and Nineteenth-Century Science: The Make-Believe of a Beginning*. Cambridge: Cambridge UP, 1984.

Stephen, Leslie, *George Eliot*. English Men of Letters. London: Macmillan, 1902.

Thale, Jerome, *The Novels of George Eliot*. New York: Columbia UP, 1959.

Williams, Raymond, *The Country and the City*. London: Chatto & Windus, 1973, 165–81.

Witemeyer, Hugh, *George Eliot and the Visual Arts*. New Haven: Yale UP, 1979.

(*d*)   Collections

Carroll, David, ed., *George Eliot: The Critical Heritage*. London: Routledge & Kegan Paul, 1971. The sixty-nine items are mainly British and American reviews of the George Eliot novels written shortly after their publication. Includes much of Henry James's criticism.

Creeger, George R., ed., *George Eliot: A Collection of Critical Essays*. Englewood Cliffs, NJ: Prentice-Hall, 1970. Reprints ten essays, including Pinney's 'The Authority of the Past in George Eliot's Novels'.

Haight, Gordon S., ed., *A Century of George Eliot Criticism*. Boston: Houghton Mifflin, 1965. Wide-ranging selections, from contemporary reviews to the early 1960s.

Haight, Gordon S., and Rosemary VanArsdel, eds, *George Eliot: A Centenary Tribute*. London: Macmillan, 1982.

Hardy, Barbara, ed., *Critical Essays on George Eliot*. London: Routledge & Kegan Paul, 1970.

Holmstrom, John and Laurence Lerner, eds, *George Eliot and her Readers: A Selection of Contemporary Reviews*. London: Bodley Head, 1966.

Knoepflmacher, U.C. and George Levine, eds, *Nineteenth-Century Fiction* (special issue: *George Eliot: 1880–1980*) 35 (1980): 253–455.

Smith, Anne, ed., *George Eliot: Centenary Essays and an Unpublished Fragment*. London: Vision, 1980.

(*e*)   Studies of Individual Works

Scenes of Clerical Life

Lodge, David, 'Introduction' to the Penguin English Library edition. 9–32.

Noble, Thomas, *George Eliot's 'Scenes of Clerical Life'*. New Haven: Yale UP, 1965.

Oldfield, Derek and Sybil, '*Scenes of Clerical Life*: The Diagram and the Picture'. Hardy, *Critical Essays*. 1–18.

Adam Bede

Clayton, Jay. 'Visionary Power and Narrative Form: Wordsworth and

Adam Bede'. ELH 46 (1979): 645–72.

Goode, John, '*Adam Bede'.* Hardy, *Critical Essays.* 19–41.

Gregor, Ian, 'The Two Worlds of *Adam Bede* (1859)'. *The Moral and the Story.* Ian Gregor and Brian Nicholas. London: Faber & Faber, 1962. 13–32.

The Mill on the Floss

Arac, Jonathan, 'Rhetoric and Realism in Nineteenth-Century Fiction: Hyperbole in *The Mill on the Floss'. ELH* 46 (1979): 673–92.

Ashton, Rosemary, '*The Mill on the Floss'*: *A Natural History.* Boston: Twayne, 1990.

Hardy, Barbara, '*The Mill on the Floss'.* Hardy, *Critical Essays.* 42–58.

McSweeney, Kerry, 'The Ending of *The Mill on the Floss'. English Studies in Canada* 12 (1986): 55–68.

Silas Marner

Carroll, David, '*Silas Marner*: Reversing the Oracles of Religion'. *Literary Monographs* 1 (1967): 167–200.

Leavis, Q.D., 'Introduction' to the Penguin English Library edition, 7–43.

Preston, John, 'The Community of the Novel: *Silas Marner'. Comparative Criticism: A Yearbook* 2 (1980): 109–30.

Simpson, Peter, 'Crisis and Recovery: Eliot, Wordsworth, and *Silas Marner'. University of Toronto Quarterly* 48 (1978/9): 95–113.

Romola

Levine, George, '*Romola* as Fable'. Hardy, *Critical Essays.* 78–98.

Robinson, Carole, '*Romola*: A Reading of the Novel'. *Victorian Studies* 6 (1962): 29–42.

Sanders, Andrew, *The Victorian Historical Novel 1840–1880.* London: Macmillan, 1978, 168–96.

Felix Holt

Coveney, Peter, 'Introduction' to the Penguin English Library edition, 7–65.

Gallagher, Catherine, 'The Failure of Realism: *Felix Holt'. Nineteenth-Century Fiction* 35 (1980): 372–84.

Kettle, Arnold, '*Felix Holt the Radical'.* Hardy, *Critical Essays,* 99–115.

Pykett, Lyn, 'George Eliot and Arnold: The Narrator's Voice and Ideology in *Felix Holt the Radical'. Literature and History* 11 (1985): 229–40.

Middlemarch

Adam, Ian, ed., *This Particular Web: Essays on 'Middlemarch'.* Toronto: U of Toronto P, 1975.

Beaty, Jerome, *'Middlemarch' from Notebook to Novel: A Study of George Eliot's Creative Method.* Urbana: U of Illinois P. 1960.

Bloom, Harold, ed., *George Eliot's 'Middlemarch'.* Moderrn Critical Interpretations. New York: Chelsea House, 1987. Reprints seven essays, including Kathleen Blake's *'Middlemarch* and the Woman Question' and Hillis Miller's 'Optic and Semiotic in *Middlemarch'.*

Daiches, David, *George Eliot: 'Middlemarch'*. Studies in English Literature. London: Edward Arnold, 1963.

Hardy, Barbara, ed., *'Middlemarch': Critical Approaches to the Novel*. London: Athlone, 1967. Eight original essays, including Mark Schorer's 'The Structure of the Novel: Method, Metaphor, and Mind'.

McSweeney, Kerry, *'Middlemarch'*. Unwin Critical Library. London: Allen & Unwin, 1984.

Daniel Deronda

James, Henry, '*Daniel Deronda*: A Conversation'. Carroll, *Critical Heritage*: 417–33.

Leavis, F.R., 'George Eliot's Zionist Novel'. *Commentary* 30 (1960): 317–25.

Levine, George, 'George Eliot's Hypothesis of Reality'. *Nineteenth-Century Fiction* 35 (1980): 1–28.

Newton, K.M., '*Daniel Deronda* and Circumcision'. *Essays in Criticism* 31 (1981): 313–27.

Shaffer, E.S., *'Kubla Khan' and 'The Fall of Jerusalem': The Mythological School in Biblical Criticism and Secular Literature 1770–1880*. Cambridge: Cambridge UP, 1975. 225–91.

Shalvi, Alice, ed., *'Daniel Deronda': A Centenary Symposium*. Jerusalem: Jerusalem Academic Press, 1976.

Index